MORE THAN
INTUITION

*My personal experience of the
ascension process*

TARRA LOGAN

BALBOA
PRESS

A DIVISION OF HAY HOUSE

Balboa Press books may be ordered through booksellers or by contacting:

Balboa Press
A Division of Hay House
1663 Liberty Drive
Bloomington, IN 47403
www.balboapress.com
1 (877) 407-4847

Print information available on the last page.

ISBN: 978-1-5043-6528-4 (sc)
ISBN: 978-1-5043-6545-1 (e)

Balboa Press rev. date: 09/20/2016

DEDICATION

I write this to honour my parents, Margaret, for her amazing determination and strength to live the life she chose for herself. She often had to face adversity with a heavy hand. She outgrew an illness that plagued her during her young adult years and exceeded the life expectancy her Doctors predicted by 50 years.

I take my hat off to my father, Evan, for his stamina in dealing with the challenges he had to overcome. I didn't know the extent of his disability until twenty-five years after his death. He was an intelligent and sensitive man who was always aware that he didn't fully understand. Every day he lived, no matter how he lived was a personal triumph.

"We never touch people so lightly that we do not leave a trace."
Peggy Tabor Millin

ACKNOWLEDGEMENTS

To everyone I have ever met and am yet to meet. To all of those who love me; ignore me; fight me; challenge me; hate me; avoid me; work with me; play with me; teach me – I thank you for all that I have gained from our interactions and the positive impact they have had on my life.

A special thanks to Caz Greene for sharing her skills with me and supporting me in this endeavour.

Throughout this book I have tried to honour everyone's privacy however, I do not live in a vacuum so to those whose first names or stories I have used I thank you for the clarity they bring to my process.

Finally I thank my brothers and sisters for being a part of my life.

Tarra

CONTENTS

PART THREE

INTRODUCTION

This book is intended to offer comfort to those individuals newly awakened to the fact that they are on the never-ending path to ascension. Sometimes it can be a lonely journey because at certain points along the way I found even those I could normally talk to about the subject were not necessarily on a similar wave length to me much of the time. That is not surprising because there are as many pathways to ascension as there are entities in the Universe. Others are so far along on their path that their knowledge and achievements can be daunting to the newly awakened.

In this book I describe some of my communications with friends, insights, aha moments, defining moments, challenges, angers, thoughts, experiences, and struggles. I have also received permission from my friend, Caz Greene, to include transcripts of some of the channels she did for and with me. Added is a little of my amateur scientific speculation to show how my mind interprets what 'my toddler' on the ascension path's perception of the universe is. Everything that I write about here is my experiences, my thoughts and as such is a true representation of what I was thinking and feeling at those times. They are not intended to imply scientific truth or historical fact, just the truth of my personal process.

Like the three blind men when asked to describe an elephant. The one encountering the elephant's tail said "an elephant resembles a rope". The second encountering a leg said "the elephant is like the trunk of a tree". The third feeling the breeze from the elephant's waving ear, felt it and said "the elephant is like a fan". The three men were correct from their point of view and so it is with us, everyone sees life through their own eyes from their perspective.

Some of my thoughts and conclusions may seem silly to you and what works for me may not work for you. The ascension process necessitates delving deep into the very core of our being through the many layers and veils that separate us from our true selves. Facing ourselves can be scary; becoming all that we can be, can be scary; letting go of things, relationships and beliefs can also be scary. Holding to our personal truth and integrity in the face of the disapproval of those nearest and dearest to us can fracture our hearts. Being great? We are already great. Not just some of us but all of us. That's the scariest thing of all to accept. Odd isn't it that most human beings are afraid of the power of their true self?

I have no miracles to relate here however, the fact that any of us exist at all is a miracle. These are the musings of my 'spiritual baby-self' being birthed from duality into a life of reality and as such is a journey of changing perceptions and increased awareness. I am a 'spiritual toddler' who just happens to be creating her new reality as a 'divine human being' here on our beloved planet Gaia.

I felt very alone at times and know others out there have similar feelings of isolation; of not being understood; of not being heard; of not even being seen. Finally we actually rise above this and know that we are never alone, surrounded as we are at all times by entities who love us unconditionally.

PART ONE

CHAPTER 1

MEMORIES

Memories appear most of the time with total recall and at other times there are the types of memories, like the one I am about to relate to you, which surface a little at a time. The following is my very first memory half of which I remembered all of my life up to the point where I am being trundled down the stairs in my stroller. The remainder suddenly surfaced when I was twenty-six years old and it actually felt like it was an idle daydream rather than a memory. I believe I recalled the second stage of the memory because the outcome of the incident remained hidden from me and I needed to know what had happened.

So, my earliest memories were of my mother trundling me down the steps of her friend's house in my stroller. The stairway, hugging the outside of the building, had its own corrugated iron roof. As we went down Mum was apologizing to her friend and the downstairs neighbour. She had been running a bath, and forgetting she was doing so, had overflowed the tub showering the downstairs flat with water. Still, I remember laughter and the atmosphere was light-hearted and pleasant.

We were going down for a walk on the beach which was just across the street from the house. Our outing consisted of me sitting in my stroller while my big brother Graham and his friend played. I would gaze out to sea while my mother and her friend talked. We used to stand (or in my case sit) under the leafy, wide spreading branches of a very large tree that grew just on the beach.

This particular day I remember that the tide was out and the toddlers were both on top of the slide. One toddler was holding the other by the ankles preparing to let him go head first down the slide. At the bottom of the slide was a big block of cement that anchored the metal posts of the slide into the sand. With the outgoing tide the ragged edges of the cement were exposed above the sand. There was a feeling of panicked concern attached to this scene.

I could hear my mother and her friend still talking and I could see little feet in white socks and shoes and the handle of the stroller. There was a tiny hand, which seemed to be disembodied, reaching up and pulling the full skirt of a dress. To the right I could see the legs and shoes of the wearer of that dress. To the left was the wide girthed trunk of the shade tree.

That is where the memory ends. My husband and I were living overseas when I put all of this together and realized it might be a memory and that the little hand might be mine. When we arrived back in Australia two years later I thought to relate this story to my mother and to ask if they were memories of an actual event. Her reaction was stunned to say the least. She said "You couldn't possibly remember that! You weren't even talking when we left Tin Can Bay!" I answered, "Well, if it is an accurate memory then apparently I can and do. I'm just as surprised as you are but what I really want to know is - did you get to the toddlers in time?" To which she replied "Yes, we did."

It turns out that I was less than eight months old when we left Tin Can Bay and this incident took place well before that. At that stage I was neither walking nor talking. My brother would have been about two and a half years old.

For me there is a moral certainty to this story, apart from respecting the potential of the individual who is a baby, we need to understand that they are born with an already well developed intelligence. My baby self knew: -

1. what it meant to overflow the bath;
2. what my mother was apologizing for and why;
3. exactly what everyone was saying, and why;

4. that what the toddlers were doing on the slippery slide was dangerous, and why;
5. how to get someone's attention and attempt to warn them;
6. what the mood and general atmosphere was like

Here's the thing though, most of us go through life unknowingly downplaying children's intelligence and natural instincts. We do this by our behaviour which shows clearly what our expectations of the child are from the day it is born and often our over-caring nature can be stifling to their normal speed of development which is very rapid in the early formative years.

I have always been fascinated by new born babies and their first reaction to the new people and things they see. How much memory of home do they retain after their birth? How much of what they already know is genetically instilled in them from their ancestral line? How much of their nature is instinctive and how much is gained from experiences of what we call 'past lives'. How much of their communication with us is telepathic and of course, ours with them? And, how much of what they think and do is divinely guided because their connection to home is still very strong?

My baby self may not have had the words to express herself but my memory retained not only an accurate picture of what happened but also the feelings accompanying the incident. My baby self also saw physical danger and attempted to warn someone of it. My mother didn't know that I was warning her but by pulling her dress perhaps I succeeded in drawing her attention away from the conversation to what was happening around her.

Why didn't I recall the final stage of the memory? I can only speculate that either my view was blocked by the two parents running to the slide and/or because the danger had passed. I don't really know and I don't know why I recalled some of that particular memory in stages.

The fact that we have memories like this provides us with valuable insights into our interactions with others. Some of course are a bit disconcerting. Have you ever said a friendly hello to a baby in its mother's arms? Usually the baby will gurgle and smile but sometimes it is shocked and cries loudly while turning its head into its mothers shoulder? This has happened to me a couple of times during my life and, knowing what I know of the intelligence of young babies, I have found those encounters to be some of the most disturbing. I come away from an experience like that feeling like I want to cry myself.

I see childhood a little like a long apprenticeship and it would be lovely to instill in our very young a sense of joy and passion for everything they do. I know as a child when I found something I loved to do I would become addicted and my joy and passion sustained me. At those times I was following my heart.

During my life there have been many pleasant memories that I like to relive and many traumatic ones that are painful to recall and fervently wish I could forget. We have our ups and downs experientially and no matter what the emotion, be it joy or sadness, at each turn we are always learning and growing. After all that is what life is all about, isn't it? I like to buoy myself up by seeing this learning cycle like an ascending spiral of steps and as I take each one I learn more and more about myself. I feel there is no need to retrace my steps; I am always walking a new path because I carry with me on the new cycle things I have learnt from the last. So even when there are issues created from an earlier cycle I need not undo what I have learnt in order to correct that issue. In fact the knowledge gained from subsequent cycles allows me to be aware that negative issues arising from previous cycles are able to be healed right back to their source simply by acknowledging them.

CHAPTER 2

DEFINING MOMENTS

"The range of what we think and do is limited by what we fail to notice. And because we fail to notice that we fail to notice, there is little we can do to change; until we notice how failing to notice shapes our thoughts and deeds."

R. D. Laing

While we are experiencing life there are many moments that propel us forward in some areas of our development while at the same time causing us to stagnate in others. The following is the first one of these that I experienced in this lifetime. I first wrote of it in 2004.

I want to acknowledge the many characters I have been along my path of ascension. Some of them I already know. The majority however, are like wisps of mist within my memory that I can't quite grasp. Still others are confined to my sub-conscious giving me, from time to time, insights into things I had no idea I knew.

There is a plethora of self-help material on the market that can assist us when we are trying to understand ourselves and these are great as guidelines to kick start our process and guide us to what we believe to be our next step. We can be helped immensely by these and grow exponentially by using the many methods and guidelines others found useful to help us along on our pathway of ascension. Then eventually, while staying open to the insights and discoveries of others, we find ourselves following our own path and for this we must look within to determine our unique purpose.

In relating this story my focus is meant to give me clarity, and to offer the seeker companionship as they navigate their journey of ascension, by sharing just one of my 'Defining Moments'. I'm referring to the points we reach that propel us to consciously take the next step to reclaim the greatness of who we really are. While each journey is unique there are similarities that others can relate to which help us to feel less lonely while navigating our personal process. I have learnt the hard way that it is detrimental to our continued development to judge ourselves when we fall short of who we think we should be. We learn from trial and error however there is also a karmic nature to some of our lessons. It is always a good thing to remind ourselves at these times that the same energies are available for all of us to utilize and on our path we begin to do just that. Used with loving intent they are very powerful indeed.

This story is about the defining moment in my life that made me question my own responses. Why I felt the way I did? Why I did things the way I did? What made me open up to or withdraw from life? Why society operated the way it did? Why beliefs and practices seemed to be contradictory? For me the dramas, traumas, and joys of daily life were secondary to the answers to these questions and many others. To tell you this I must first give you a little background about my early childhood.

I was born on 20 April, 1950 and during the first eight years of my life I had a relatively normal childhood for the 1950's. In our household there were the usual chores to do. We had a variety of pets including dogs, cats, roosters, and chickens. We sometimes had pet joeys that Dad had rescued from the pouch of a kangaroo that had been hit by a car. My mother always had finches and budgerigars and often injured wild birds that she rescued and was nursing back to health. The joeys and injured birds were released back into the wild when it was deemed they were able to take care of themselves.

We lived in Queensland towns moving every year to follow the assigned logging trail that was Dad's Job most of the time. By the time I was eight we had lived in six different towns, one of them twice, we had lived in eleven different houses and one four-man tent.

Mum was a dressmaker, working from home while she looked after her four children. Our youngest brother Timothy did not share any of our early life because he was born much later in 1968. In fact, Mum gave birth to him five days after I was married. During the school holidays we would travel with Mum by train to visit our grandparents' farms while Dad stayed behind to continue working. We learnt to ride horses and to round-up and milk cattle. When Graham was five years old Uncle Peter, while keeping pace alongside the little blue Ransom tractor, taught him to drive. It didn't take long before Graham was able to take the cream cans down to the gate for collection. We had the usual stilts, soap-boxes, push-bikes, tennis rackets, cricket equipment, reel fishing lines, toy pianos, fifes, mouth organs, yoyos, swings etc, and could use all of these - some more successfully than others. We learnt to dog paddle in the creeks rather than in a swimming pool because none of the towns where we lived had one.

All of the above was normal for the 1950's. Added to this and our Sunday school lessons and schoolwork though was another layer of practical knowledge gained from my grandparents' and parent's experiences during the depression of the early 1900's and during World War I & II. Our parents wanted us to be capable of looking after ourselves if suddenly we found we were alone in the sometimes harsh countryside of Australia.

I remember Dad stopping in a very dry area and showing us how to extract moisture from various cacti and the fruit of one in particular that was safe to eat. He showed us the most likely spots to look for water by digging down to the moisture level and allowing the hole to fill through seepage. It takes quite a while to fill the hole and when the water arrives it is sort of murky and frothy. We were shown how to peel and cook fresh water eels, to fish, catch crabs, and dig for yabbies in the mud of a drying waterhole or dam, and how to make fire without matches. That took me forever. I can't remember if I ever got past producing smoke. We were shown what wood to collect for a smokeless fire and how to set one, how to bake fish, potatoes, and damper in the ashes under the coals of a bush fire. We were shown how to tie and use a lasso; to throw a boomerang although I never attempted to catch a returning one but I remember Graham doing so at least once; how to crack a whip; to make and use a sling shot; to make and fly a kite; and to shoot an air rifle at tin cans with great accuracy. We assisted with Dad's vegetable patch when he had one and were sometimes more of a hindrance than a help.

I learnt from my brother Graham how to chop wood and kindling for our stove and how to sharpen the push mower blades. My Uncles and Aunts showed us where to find wild gooseberries and other berries; how to cook bunya nuts; and render fat down to dripping. My mother taught us how to make cough syrup and when we had colds we always had the mixture slow cooking on the side of the wood stove.

The recipe was simple:-

COUGH SYRUP

In a small stainless steel saucepan place 2 finely chopped onions and 1 cup of sugar. Pour in 1 ½ cups of water and bring to boil. Reduce temperature to a slow simmer. Simmer for 15 minutes (or longer if necessary). If you are lucky enough to have a combustion or ordinary wood stove move saucepan to the side of the range to keep it warm. You now have syrup that soothes the throat better than any cough syrup I've ever used and the onion boosts the immune system at the same time. Administer a teaspoon to the patient periodically until the cough subsides.

Mum also taught Graham, our younger sister Heather, and I how to make toys, mend, sew, knit, light the stove, cook, wash, turn cartwheels, make Christmas decorations, and play lots of fun games. She loved to sing and taught us many modern and old songs from our Grandparents time. Dad could play any tune by ear and at night would play for us on his guitar or harmonica. When our young brother Evan was born we learnt, as older siblings do, how to care for a young baby too.

All of the above sounds intense but it wasn't ever made obvious that we were being taught and was introduced to us as the opportunities arose during our travels. Can I do any of this now? Most of it yes, and others with a little thought and practice I could do again. What was important to our parents was that we could do them then while we were very young.

There were very few things I needed to question at this point although my opinions were quite different from others at times. There were of course the normal family dramas and we children weren't always little angels. We all had plenty of time on our hands because TV reception wasn't available out west where we were living until 1960. I didn't really begin to question the things adults were saying until I went to school and Sunday school.

I remember one day in 1957, when we were living in Wondai, two Aborigine boys were put in my class. They were much taller and therefore I assumed much older than us and were both afraid and became physically sick. When I went home that afternoon, frustrated, I said to my mother "Why is the school doing this? Don't they know that Aborigines don't like a roof over their heads? Why don't they just leave them alone to do things in their own time? It's going to take much longer than this" (A 7 year olds view of the situation). My mother didn't answer and I found out much later that she knew it was the wrong thing to do but didn't know what the right thing to do was, so she had no answer to give me. The boys were there the next day and the same thing happened. The following day they were gone so I assumed the teachers must have come to the same conclusion that I had.

Please understand that I know that many Aborigines had lived or worked in western style houses for almost a century by the mid to late 1950's but this state was enforced by our society. Many were dispossessed of their traditional stamping grounds; their culture ignored; forbidden to speak their own language they lived like ghosts mostly ignored on the fringes of towns they passed in their roaming. In the towns where we lived the local Aborigines were still very much nomadic and when they were in

9

town they often camped out in the show grounds where there were toilets, water tanks, and shelter in the stands from the elements. The stands had no walls or doors so opened onto the countryside and the fresh air which suited their life style reasonably well.

A child of the 50's yearned to be outdoors and if permitted only ever went into the house to do set chores, or at sundown to do homework, and to eat and sleep. I envied the lifestyle that the Aborigines preferred even though at that young age I was painfully aware of their collective sadness.

We moved to Chinchilla and one day when plans were being made for the church Christmas play I refused to be a part of it. I told them that in Sunday School we were taught that it was wrong to pretend we were someone we were not. That was the first time I decided to do something to make a point. What can I say? I was eight years old! I was becoming increasingly disillusioned with the powers to be (adults in this case) for their hypocrisy. They were forever telling children not to do certain things because it was a sin and then they would go right ahead and do those same things themselves. So, I stood up to the institution where right and wrong was taught. Children often see things as black or white. In the 1950's so did our society – at least for the children it did. Up to this point in my life things were following a normal pattern with a little rebellion beginning to show. I tell you now of the following incident to demonstrate how a defining moment can appear to be an incident that would normally be shrugged off as inconsequential against the background I've just outlined.

'My class was out on a field trip. We were on foot and had reached the outskirts of Chinchilla when my friend pointed out her house to the teacher and said "That's where I live." It was a small grey weather board house that had never been painted. The unfenced yard was littered with the skeletons of tricycles, an old pram, a push mower and a pile of planks with long grass growing up through and around it, toys and a tin bucket or two. I had visited my friend there many times and it was a wonderful yard to play in. I whispered to my friend "Why did you tell her where you live?" I was embarrassed for

her and shocked by the fact. Thankfully, she just looked at me not understanding the question and I didn't/couldn't explain it anyway.'

For the rest of that day and until now my reaction has never left my memory. I don't agonize over it anymore of course – what's done is done. I had never felt embarrassment before with such intensity. The humiliation I felt as a result of my reaction was severe. I had never felt my stomach churn and rise in my throat as it did then bringing tears of shame to my eyes.

The questions that assaulted my mind were difficult for an eight year old to handle. Not why was I embarrassed for my friend but why did I feel embarrassment at all? How did I know about shame? Where had these feelings come from? They were not based on anything in my experience up to that point in my life. AND, what business of mine was it anyway? My family didn't even own a house. Where did these intense reactions come from? There was nothing in my short past to explain it and my reaction left me very confused and physically ill.

This single incident opened me up to questioning myself and at the same time closed me off to reaching out to others, not because others couldn't be trusted but, because I felt I could no longer trust myself to interact freely with them. To a large degree I lost my spontaneity that day and along with it my lighthearted approach to life over a reaction I felt powerless to control. I also found that I had strange values that I wasn't consciously aware of before. And too, I had suddenly come to the realization that words had power beyond what I had understood not just over others but over myself and I wasn't sure I was equipped to handle it. I certainly didn't feel equipped to handle the effects of such intense emotions on my physical body.

I was confused by the fact that my reactions felt like they came from past memories – but they were memories I knew I didn't have – at least not in my current life. This is when my understanding of reincarnation began to surface but I didn't consciously know about the word nor did I entertain the possibility of the concept until almost a decade later. I had literally pushed the idea aside refusing to acknowledge it.

On the negative side, I became emotionally paralyzed and that side of my nature became hopelessly underdeveloped. I still do not share my emotions with others with ease. On the positive side this simple slip-up could have easily remained just that and I could have shrugged it off and would have but for my intense reaction to it. A thirty second window of opportunity to learn opened for me that day and I was lucky enough to recognize it. I'm sure I have missed many in the ensuing years but am grateful that I didn't miss that one despite its repercussions.

This incident set me on a path to learn more about myself and while there have been many more defining moments in my life, there have been none as emotionally traumatic or pivotal as that first one. At those subsequent times I learnt more about myself and my awareness expanded to encompass more knowledge of what is available to us. I also began the long journey of learning to accept myself as a human being who makes mistakes like anyone else.

There is a deeper meaning to this particular defining moment as I'm sure you can see. The incident was a simple trigger for me to recognize false values I brought through to this life to work on. I have had other triggers like this since which were equally easy for me to recognize. I won't relate the whole story here because it involves another person who I had agreed to work with during this life time.

When I was fourteen I went to a country show which was crammed with people. I was just walking around looking at the exhibits when, without any fanfare or warning, my attention was drawn across to the other side of the show grounds to one person who had his back to me. It was like I had tunnel vision, where the distance between me and this person was stage lit and the remainder of the scene faded into the shadows of my periphery vision as did all sound too. I didn't make contact then but did a few months later through a mutual friend. There were things that each of us needed to learn from one another and through a long association, we did.

The way these triggers work for me is by drawing my focus to the target, be it a person or incident, to the exclusion of all else that is happening around me.

For a moment I want to refer back to my comment about standing up to the powers that be in my day in 1958, and letting them know what I thought about their double standards. As I watch what children and young teenagers around the world are doing today I see the new world that they are intentionally creating for themselves despite the organizations and governing bodies around the globe. It's now 2008 and the children are in turn addressing you and me as we addressed the adults of our day. They are speaking of deeper issues with more elegance and greater effect than I had the knowledge or courage to do. In the majority of cases we, the adults who spoke out when we were children, haven't moved forward in that many of us haven't taken a stand about what we will and will not accept. It is not too late to hear and act on the wisdom of the children or to support them in their endeavors. They are saying what many of us have been thinking over the years drawing the conclusion that in far too many cases our government representatives and world leaders can not or will not represent us with integrity.

Quite a while back my attention was drawn to an incident that took place when a teenager representing a group called ECO addressed the U N. If you would like to listen on utube it will only take 10 minutes of your time (Google 'Teenager Address UN Summit 1992'). The content of the speech impressed me however what impressed me more was that the Conference heard her as evidenced by the effect her words had on the people in the room. After this girl's address the assemblage was silent for a full five minutes – there wasn't a sound in the room – they were stunned because what she said was true they didn't have answers. What was more important though is that it was transparently obvious to the world they represent that the world knew that they didn't have answers.

The second thing that I want to acknowledge is that thankfully, these days we have become appreciative and respectful of the Australian Aborigines Culture and their many and varied artistic abilities. Many of us are also willing to learn from their ancient wisdom particularly in relation to natural medicines and caring for Mother Earth. I have been waiting to see this happen on a recognizable scale since I was eight years old but like my mother had no answers and knew that spiritual evolution of the western race was the key to accepting and embracing our differences. Perhaps I have also come to understand why the Aborigines didn't like a roof over their heads. The obvious part of this is the heaviness of the air in a house no matter how many windows and doors are open and how strong the breeze is blowing through the house. What was not obvious to me when I was younger was the grounding experienced by an individual when walking barefoot on mother earth. Most children instinctively feel this and prefer to be barefoot.

The third is that curiosity was probably aroused by my mention of living in a tent. Actually, our time in the tent was an experience that stays pleasantly in my memory. When we moved to Wondai there were no houses for rent so, through necessity and until one became available, the Council allowed us to pitch a tent just inside the back gate of the show grounds. It was quite a hike to the toilet which we all visited in the morning before going to work and school. We children made sure we visited the toilet at school, the picture theatre, or church before going home again too. Of course, during the night there was no way that we would traipse down to the toilet. We were mindful of the snakes and red backs. I was also scared of the dark. Like every family did during the magnificent time of the 'thunder box' we brought the pot into service at night.

A four-man tent is quite big and the head space is quite high at the center of the tent so it never did feel cramped and canvas is surprisingly cool in summer and warm in winter. Mum and Dad pulled everything we needed out of storage. Dad drove his green utility into the back left hand quarter of the tent. The 'Ute' had a covered back, like a gypsy caravan, so we children hung our clothes from the ribbing around the inside of that. Dad put a single mattress in its tray and Mum made up the bed. That room became Heathers and mine giving us warmth, comfort and privacy. Over the packed earth of the remainder of the tent they put down newspaper and then placed their precious rolls of linoleum over that. (Rental houses didn't have floor coverings in the 1950's. We had to provide our own which we rolled up and packed to take with us when we moved on.) In the back right hand quarter of the tent was Graham's camp stretcher, Mum's sewing machine, and a chest of drawers to store the folded clothes in. Mum and Dad put their bed, Evan's cot, and their wardrobe in the front left quarter of the tent. The wardrobe became a wall giving them privacy. In the right front quarter of the tent was the kitchen with our kerosene fridge, the kitchen cabinet, a small table with two prymus' for cooking, a camp table and canvas chairs. Our lighting was two kerosene lamps one of which hung on a long hook from the ribbing of the canvas roof and the other remained portable to be used inside and out as needed.

Our water supply was from the tank at the stands in the grounds. Dad would collect water with his truck and fill the drums we had next to the tent. During the 50's and even early 60's most houses we rented in country towns did not have bathrooms or toilets inside. One visited the outhouse (thunder box) to go to the toilet and the washhouse (laundry) to have a bath in an iron tub. Having a bath was really no different from having one in a house. We used the big iron tub and cold water heated with two kettles of boiling water. When we children had a bath no-one left the tent. Mum had hers before we came home from school and we all moved outside while Dad had his – simple!

Mum's two washing lines were hung out between three trees and we had a big fire pit over which she boiled the clothes in her copper. So on wash day we had the most amazing food you have ever tasted baked in the coals from those fires. In winter we would heat our bricks in the coals too and then roll them in a clean potato sack to warm our feet at night. One night Graham put his brick in the bed earlier because it had been cold the night before. While we were having our evening cocoa we smelt something burning. The smoke had just begun to rise through his blankets. He rushed over and pulled the smoking sack out and tossed it out through the flap of the tent. Luckily it was only the sack that had begun to burn. He put the sack on the fire, cooled his brick down a little, found a new sack, and returned it to his now toasty warm bed. We were all much more careful after that.

You would think Mum had enough to do caring for four children, her husband, and dressmaking under those conditions. Of course she did. One day Heather and I came home from school upset because all of our friends had chips from the fish and chip shop. They weren't rolled in butcher's paper or newspaper they were in little grease proof bags – the new thing. We had little money at that time so couldn't ever afford to do that. Mum didn't say anything but told us to come home for lunch the next day. When we arrived home she gave us a drink of cold cocoa made with milk and when we finished that she handed each of us chips in little grease proof bags that she had made on her sewing machine from grease proof lunch wrap. We walked back to school eating our crisp home made chips. The best of all though was when I looked over at my sister and could see that she was puffed up and walking on air just like I was.

I heartily thank Mum and Dad for the memories.

CHAPTER 3

ENDINGS AND NEW BEGINNINGS

"Remember that there is nothing stable in human affairs; therefore avoid undue elation in prosperity, or undue depression in adversity."

Socrates

My attention was drawn screaming back to family matters in the latter part of 1959 when my parent's fifteen year relationship ended. Dad was compelled to go his own way and we eventually went to live with a man and his two daughters and became a family of sorts. I thought my heart could not break anymore but I was wrong. Early the following year our family took another blow when, at the insistence of Mums partner, we three older children were sent to live with our father leaving our younger brother Evan behind. We all had to go to school and couldn't do that and care for a toddler too. Within a month the family was fragmented further when Graham now fourteen decided to leave school and go out to work on a farm. He only came home on weekends. Heather and I mechanically went to school, ran the house, and escaped into outdoor activities – swimming in the local creek; visiting friends; walking on the railway sidings on our stilts; and playing tennis on the school tennis court during the weekends. At night I cooked dinner with Heather's help. She was too young to use a sharp knife but could use a potato peeler. After dinner we'd wash up, bathe, do our homework, and watch TV or listen to Graham's records. On Saturday nights, in the town hall just across the street from us, there were often dances and traveling entertainers like Rick & Thel Carey, Chad Morgan, and others. Heather and I went to all of those. Admission was free for children. Even with all of this activity it took me several months to pull myself out of the robotic state I found myself in.

As I became aware of my general surroundings again my childhood ended and my teenage years began. I went into action and with Heather's help cleaned the house out more thoroughly and in this way we made the final move into our father's house in Cooyar and adopted a new way of being. Before the year was out we moved to Crows Nest and Graham joined us there to work on Perseverance Dam with Dad. We moved on to Imbil after this and Graham left again to work out west. I left school at the end of 1964 knowing full well that the endowment I'd used thus far would not be sufficient to see me through the remainder of my secondary education. I went out to work and Graham came and collected Heather insisting she move back with Mum, who was now in Toowoomba, and continue her education there. After a few months I joined them having discovered that I didn't like the job I was doing.

While I loved my father I was unable to let go of the reins during our time with him and barely moved out of survival mode during those three years. When I returned to Mum's house there was only Mum, Heather, and Evan living there. Mum's partner and Graham were working in different towns further out west and only returned periodically. Mum's partner's two daughters had grown up and left home by then too. I finally felt free to release the reins, relax and breathe again. Soon after this I had my fifteenth birthday and this marked the beginning of my adulthood.

I found a job and paid Mum for my board but it was not sufficient to support all of us. A few months later, having received no financial support from her partner for some time, Mum went out to work. I soon began to date several older teenage boys liking one in particular who eventually became my regular boyfriend. To tie up a loose end in the story here I should tell you that this boyfriend is the person I saw in the distance at the country show.

Approximately two years later we became engaged when I was seventeen and he was twenty. Six months later we moved to Atherton. Six months later we were married in Townsville; I was eighteen and Keith was twenty-one. Nine months later we became pregnant and four months later we lost the baby and our adult hearts broke. The pregnancy wasn't planned although we both thought we would eventually have a family. Our miscarriage put the possibility in a different light and we took steps to prevent any further pregnancies thus ended our traditional marriage and a new phase of our adult life began.

Experiences were what we became interested in. We began to travel and work overseas, the first time in the 1970's for four years. We went via Singapore, Delhi, and Northern India then spent three years in Katmandu and six months in Edinburgh. Keith took extended long service leave and we traveled for six months through Great Britain, Europe, the United States, and Israel. On our return to Australia we felt a need to put down roots for a time and brought a house and concentrated on our various interests and careers. In the 1980's we went overseas again for two years; this time to Nanning in Guangxi Zuan Autonomous Region in mainland China. We spent our annual leave in Hong Kong, Macao, and Guangzhou. On returning to Australia we again concentrated on our various interests and careers. We had been growing apart for a number of years but like most people who have invested thirty-five years in each other (we actually met and went out on our first date when I was fourteen and he was seventeen) I had the feeling that the marriage should be saved. It was traditional to do so after all. I know better now and for me it's like any relationship - when it has run its course let it go. Keith knew this and left and five years later we divorced.

We shared many exciting, loving, sad, interesting, informative, hilarious, exotic, and erotic experiences during those many years we were together and I'm sure we learnt a lot from each other and after all, that is what relationships are all about aren't they?

Thus ended the first stage of my adult life and even though we grew apart and the break was inevitable there was a long mourning period for me to process and a new adjustment to a solitary life for a time. My companions, Tinker and Saanu who were miniature fox terriers and Sharmeli, who was a yellow budgerigar, helped me through this transition as did many of my friends and colleagues.

While initially I had some regrets about every stage of my life I have come to understand the lessons in the challenges that are sent my way. Now when challenges come up I am able to say with a large sigh and a little tired laugh or a sense of excitement "here we go again" knowing that I, as we all do, have the ability to respond. Earlier in my life I would often surprise myself when difficulties arose by saying aloud, "Ain't life grand?" not quite understanding what I really meant. I now know with certainty that each challenge brings a new opportunity to grow. I am now becoming practiced at remaining centered most of the time learning to recognize when things are over. Sometimes noticing and sometimes, as in the past, ignoring the signs and had to face the consequences of an unnecessarily prolonged process.

Now in the second stage of my adult life the urge to write this book has become so strong over the past few years that it will no longer be denied. I believe there is a need to hear an average person's thoughts and experiences no matter how silly or profound they may seem to be alongside those of professionals and those who trust their connection to source. All of us without exception have a story to tell and we do it in a multitude of ways. The majority tell their stories by the way they live their lives and others automatically learn from them without even being aware that that is what is happening. What we don't always accept is that we and our young learn from everyone we come in contact with and the behaviours and beliefs we adopt are the result of personal choice. We cannot blame those choices on influences outside ourselves and in this journey toward ascension it is impossible to succeed if we insist on doing that. The key is truth and integrity and unashamedly accepting our personal process without needing validation from others. Everyone's process is authentically their own it can be no-one else's. The ascension process is just another step in our evolution. Humanity has put it off for far too long and spiritual evolution is knocking insistently at our door.

CHAPTER 4

MOMENTS OF GREATER AWARENESS

"Do not go where the path may lead, go instead where there is no path and leave a trail."

Ralph Waldo Emerson

Times of knowing can easily be missed falling into place sometimes years later. I remember a couple of years ago during a channeling session with a friend; I said to the entities coming through "When I am fully awake I will be able to ...." The entities replied with confusion, "But you are awake." At the time I did not understand exactly what they meant. Now I do. Once we remember the truth of who we are we are awakened. Just because we don't remember all of our experiences or how to do all of the astonishing things that we are capable of, that does not mean we aren't aware that if we trust ourselves we are capable of doing them. Abilities fade when not in use or when we believe we don't have them. Like any ability when we believe in ourselves and nurture it over a period of time, that ability strengthens or in this case returns. 'Use it or lose it' is advisable for all of our senses not just the physical ones.

Like most human beings I am used to directing my life and was very attached to what I did. With spiritual abilities it is essential that we form no expectations or attachments to outcomes. I found it almost impossible to get my head around that concept at times and my heart would ache for recognizable contact to the point where I sometimes forgot the things I have felt and seen clearly. So, I remind myself from time to time and the following are some examples of heightened awareness that I think may interest the reader.

1. *I was fifteen and one day while at work and during a tea break I had a horrible unsettling feeling in the pit of my stomach that something had happened to my boyfriend. We didn't have a phone at that time and nor did he. Keith also lived over five hundred miles away from me so I only saw him on weekends. When he arrived two weeks later I remembered to ask him what had happened to him at that time on that particular day. He told me he was in a car that was following his friend's car home when his friend was involved in an accident. His friend was killed; a terrible tragedy and a terrible thing to witness for anyone let alone an eighteen year old. I have had unexplainable things like this happen before but felt that they fell more into the category of intuition. Like knowing what someone was going to say before they said it or answering someone's thoughts, surprising them and me when they would say, "How did you know I was thinking that?" At those times I hear it so clearly that I think the person has actually spoken, but they haven't! The feeling in the pit of my stomach was because I am empathic – this is not uncommon – mothers have this same connection with their children. As to hearing what people think, I don't really know what that is – could be telepathy or clairaudience – perhaps I can really hear people think sometimes like I could hear what the announcer was saying on the old TV when it was muted. In later life I had said to my husband on a number of occasions when I was trying to sleep, "Will you stop thinking so loud I'm trying to sleep." This is not uncommon either.*

2. *It is early morning and I am relieved to see our little Adelaide turtle dive off her rock and swim in the tank. She had been ill and I was happy and relieved to see her well again so went to*

tell Keith that she was fine. He cuddled me and said "no she died during the night and I buried her this morning before you woke up". This was my first memory of seeing clearly beyond the veil but at the time we didn't know that that was what had happened. I was responsible for her illness you see. We had traveled from Dalby to Atherton during a 104 F heat wave and the small amount of water she traveled with to keep her shell moist had dried up fast and her shell cracked underneath. I wasn't aware of it until we pulled into the motel that night. Despite our efforts to save her she died two days later. I was nineteen and my husband was twenty-two and we both assumed that I saw her swimming because I couldn't handle the guilt and loss. Yes, that is why I saw her but she was telling me she was ok now. It is not uncommon for animals, particularly beloved pets, to communicate through the veil from both sides in this way.

3. *After we moved from our flat in Atherton to a house on the outskirts of town I had a very unusual experience. There was a doorway in the house that I couldn't walk through just on dusk but could do so at any other time during the day or night. I would walk right up to the threshold but couldn't take a step further. I wasn't exactly frightened but my body did shake at those times because there was an energetic barrier that felt palpable to me. This happened a few times and I had to go and get Keith to get me through the doorway; once on the other side I was fine. It was the doorway to the toilet so we had to find out what was happening because the toilet was essential to my wellbeing. The house was one that had been moved and the landlord had built the extension himself adding a bathroom and a toilet with a little verandah and stairs leading down to the laundry and carport. We asked our landlord during a casual conversation (not explaining why we were curious) where he had found his building materials. He had brought them from an old saw mill that had been demolished because it was no longer in use. Keith had lived with his family in the area during his school years and related to me an incident he*

remembered when he was about fifteen. A man from the town had gone to the mill one evening and hung himself from a beam. The energetic imprint that this mans emotions left was very intense and we realized that that was what I was feeling. Once we discovered this I no longer had difficulty passing through that doorway because the intense energies were no longer there. Many souls who die traumatically often remain attached to areas, buildings, or those they love. I believe that because we felt genuine compassion and sadness for the intense emotions that caused him to end his life thus acknowledging him, we opened a love conduit or bridge for him to finally pass over. I do not know his name but feel for him and his family and friends and hope my writing about this won't upset them too much.

4. *Keith had been curious about UFO's for years but had not told me of his interest before. I was twenty when we went to visit a family who was interested in them too. Some members of the family had drawn the UFO's they had seen. Most were of the cigar shaped variety with just the outer shell but others included detailed drawings of the interiors as well. The family had formed a sort of club where like people came to compare notes and some of the other's sightings were of saucer shaped craft. I can still remember the energy that seemed to be characteristic to all of the family members we were talking to. They vibrated a little differently to my vibration so that I felt their energy as a strong vertical pressure in the center of my chest. The pressure remained for perhaps ten minutes after we left and was sufficient for me to comment on it to Keith. As we were leaving I can remember one of the men looking at us as he said you will be recognized wherever you go. Although I wondered what he meant by that statement at the time I asked no questions and thought nothing more of it until five years later when we were living in Kathmandu. An elderly lady, I knew by sight but had never met, approached me at our club one night and quietly introduced herself to me as a medium. I showed polite interest not wanting to get involved in what I thought at the time could*

be a dangerous activity in the hands of someone like me who didn't know what they were doing. In light of my polite but non-responsive reaction she didn't expand on that comment and I asked no questions of her. On a subsequent night while at the club this same lady collapsed. The people I was with did not understand why her husband said as he supported her, "She will be all right now. I'll just take her home" and refused to call a doctor as others were urging him to do. My friends thought him unfeeling but I knew what was happening and realized that many may not understand or accept her gift. I did not discuss the incident with my friends and Keith kept the confidence too. Obviously my energy suggested to her that I was ready to connect or at least be capable of connecting at that time. A window of opportunity opened and it may appear to others to be one missed but I was still fearful and therefore not ready to take that step.

5. *When I was thirty-one we were visiting relatives, when one day we were taken to meet some of their friends. We got out of the car and as we walked toward the house I got this horrible sick feeling in my stomach and throat. I stopped dead and said quietly to Keith "There's something wrong, I don't want to go in." By this time he was beginning to lose patience with me and insisted we go in. Through that whole visit the lady we were visiting barely managed to keep herself together and the emotions I was feeling from her were intense . . . . . the others seemed oblivious. At one point her husband took my friends to see some renovations he had done and I stayed with the lady. She apologized to me and said they had just had the most horrendous row and this time she realized that her marriage may not survive their differences.*

6. *I'm almost reluctant to tell you about this one but in my introduction I said I would tell you about my experiences and this one has a different tone to the others so must be included. Another incident occurred while we were staying with our relatives. Their house was an old one that they had restored themselves. One night there was a party of twelve or so people*

and at one point we happened to place our chairs around the room in a rough circle to talk. As we talked and then as I began to just listen the sounds of the music and the peoples voices began to fade away. I sat there fascinated, watching as everyone laughed and talked while I sat in my silent world. After a while I began to hear them again. As the guests were leaving I walked into the formal dining room randomly picking up items from the sideboard and putting them back down again. Then I walked to the window and closed the curtains. I thought it strange as I was doing this because it is not something I would normally do in someone else's house. We went to bed soon after that and as we lay talking my body began to shake violently and the floor length curtains suddenly blew into the room horizontally and continued to do so for several minutes. It was a still night. There wasn't even a breeze outside. Keith held me tight and insisted in the name of God that whoever it was should leave. He repeated this several times and the curtains returned to their window position in slow motion. I eventually stopped shaking. At the time I thought that this was a rather "pissed off" entity and I was surprised that it waited a week to make itself know to us. I had no idea what it wanted and I didn't feel it again during the next week of our stay. I now know that the entities attempts to contact me grew stronger and stronger that night only because I was not acknowledging it. As soon as we did that it left us alone. Did calling on God help? Yes, when Keith did that I received the protection that I was unaware I needed to provide for myself as I was beginning to connect more strongly with the other side. I have learnt that as we expand our awareness we can be contacted not only by the higher frequencies but by those who still have ego based energy. The trick is to begin by asking that only entities 'of the light' contact us for our highest good. Protection can be as easy as setting the intention to be shrouded in golden white light. Of course I wasn't intentionally contacting anyone at that time but my soul was prompting me to do so and trying to make me understand that it was time to learn about these things.

7. *Thirty-nine years old. Other experiences can be less certain and make you wonder – I did more than wonder, I actually went to get my eyes tested to see if I was developing cataracts or glaucoma. I had often seen movement out of the corner of my eye before over the years and would turn and shrug it off when I found there was no-one there. These oddities began to occur on a daily and sometimes twice daily basis but when it happened several times while I was driving I became concerned. I told the Optometrist what was happening and he checked my eyes and told me that whatever was happening it had nothing to do with my eyes. I have often read that many see the beings of the elemental kingdom in this manner at first. I don't know if that is what was happening to me at these times or if in quiet times when my mind was still I was seeing through the veil.*

8. *In my mid-forties the next notable incidents of interest would be when on three separate occasions over a period of several months, while I was driving between Brisbane and Toowoomba on the Gatton by-pass, I saw four men in a paddock working the soil with picks and shovels and three mounted horsemen were attempting to control their skittish horses while conversing with the men on the ground. They were close enough to the road that I could see the dust kicked up by the horses' hooves. There was a comfortable feeling about the encounter and the scene but I was curious about what was going on. When I pointed them out to my mother-in-law who was traveling with me and said "I wonder what those men are doing?" She looked over then back at me and asked "What men?" When I saw them the second time I had a friend with me but she couldn't see them either. The third time I was alone. I began to wonder why I was seeing the scene. I then remembered that both sets of my mother's grandparents had settled in that area soon after they came to Australia. The Logan family came over on the Montmorency in 1860 and eventually brought up farm land near Gatton in 1869. The Whittle family had a business in the township itself. I realized that they could just be family saying "Hi!" With that acknowledgement I stopped seeing this*

scene but the pleasant feeling remains every time I pass by that location.

9. One day, I had this strong urge to go out to Deception Bay to check on my mother-in-law's house. She was away for a couple of weeks. I had a key to her house but had never felt the need to check it whenever she was away before. I told myself not to be silly; she'll be home next week. The feeling persisted so I looked at the clock and decided to go. It was a two and a half hour round trip and I could be home again by midnight. As I opened the door to Mum's house her budgerigar, which had been missing for three weeks, was walking down the hall towards me. Even though she was too weak to fly she was difficult to catch because she kept running under the bed in the spare bed room. I finally caught her, gave her water and seed, put her in her small travel cage, and took her back home to Brisbane with me. When I phoned Mum she was thrilled to hear her beloved budgerigar was safe and not lost at all.

10. My friend and I were sitting in the shade out in her garden. It was late afternoon and we were enjoying the quiet and a cup of tea. While we were talking I happened to look over at her and noticed green and gold light like electric currents playing around her right elbow. I looked away and closed my eyes. No it wasn't the effects of the sun. Opening my eyes I looked back at her arm and the currents were clearly still there. I said to my friend, "You have green and gold electricity running around your right elbow." She replied, "I had a sore shoulder this morning so asked Archangel Raphael for some healing." I said, "Well he is working on your elbow." I knew that green light was used for healing but had never seen it before and was fascinated by the gold and green interplay.

11. I had just finished my exercise routine that I did every night and was standing doing some breathing exercises when my upper body began to turn to the right. I let the rest of my body follow and did a 360 degree turn then I stopped. My body had other ideas and I gave up trying to stop it after the fourth turn and counted them instead. It stopped after twelve slow 360

degree turns. At the time, I didn't know why this happened; I couldn't even guess or speculate. Later in the year while in a channeling session I happened to remember to relate this to spirit and I was told "you were tightening strands".

12. *I was sitting on a stool at the breakfast bar in my kitchen reading a book. Without planning it I began to speak out loud to spirit. I asked God, Archangel Michael, Archangel Raphael, Archangel Uriel, and Archangel Gabriel to assist me in clearing away all fears relating to giving up smoking and began to list them. Fears like becoming a pain-in-the-butt reformed smoker, getting fat, becoming bad tempered from withdrawal symptoms and as I did this great tears began to wash down my face and there was this great whoosh of energy that went straight up and out through my crown chakra. I got such a surprise that I knocked the stool over because I stood up so quickly. I heard myself saying "Oh God, what have I done, what have I done? . . . . . .". Within seconds I was over my surprise and said to all in general . . . . . "that freaked me out"! I had covered all of my bases in the ones I asked to assist me - God of course, Michael for dispelling fear, Raphael for physical healing, Uriel for clearing psychological blocks, and Gabriel to ensure my communication was effective. Powerful as they all are if I had not been sincere in my intention they could not have helped me. I had tried to give up smoking many times using patches and other techniques – nothing worked. I had been a fifteen to twenty cigarettes a day smoker for ten or more years and had just had the last one in my pack while reading my book just before I did this. I have not smoked a cigarette since then. The urge is there but my will is rock solid – the strength of will I was able to bring to bear on this issue never ceases to amaze me. It was the first time that I truly understood the phrase 'steadfast in my resolve'. This was also the first time that I felt the great power of my energies with such physical force. As to the water-fall flood of tears, it is not crying and I experience that intense release whenever I connect with spirit. It comes unbidden and it is an emotion but not the*

one you might think. It is not sadness but a taste of the joy that they bring, the feeling unrecognizable to most of us, that our physical body has difficulty containing. It makes you want to sob because it so overwhelming. It was Archangel Michael who explained this emotion as one we often don't recognize as joy. We feel great happiness but seldom experience intense joy and so often equate it to grief which we feel with equal intensity.

13. *I was using the electric typewriter, checking it out to see if it still worked before giving it away to a friend. I was copying something I wanted typed up and was on the second line when I had to stop to adjust the page I was copying from. While I was doing that the typewriter began to type on its own. Thinking I had brushed my arm across the sensitive keys as I reached over to adjust the page, I pulled the paper out of the typewriter none too gently, with a whispered curse. The correction tape was used up so I would need to begin again. I looked at the page and to my surprise this is what I read – "Hello, I'd like . . ." The words were typed exactly like that! It was obvious to me that brushing my arm across the keys could not possibly produce those words let alone the capitals and punctuation. Needless to say I have kept that page with me to this day. I thought to mention this to Quan Yin and you can read the explanation and the remainder of the message they intended to give me that day in the channel dated 31 May, 2005.*

14. *After a meditation session, where I had not relaxed sufficiently to still my mind, I got up and while walking through the house I said with frustration to Archangel Michael "when I am able to hear you the sun will be shining and the birds will be singing" as I continued on my way I put the frustration out of my mind preparatory to doing some computer work. About two minutes later I heard quite a commotion outside in the back yard. The racket persisted so I walked out the back door to see what was happening and looked up to see more than a dozen birds of various types flying really fast several times around the large gum tree just out from my back steps. They were singing away at the top of their little lungs as they did this and then they broke*

ranks flying off in separate directions. I laughed with joy and gratitude and thereafter always called that tree Michael. The tree was at least 12 meters high towering over the two stories of our house. I considered it imposing enough to be named Michael. During this period of my growth I often had 'spit the dummy' moments where I was taken away from communication with spirit. Expectations, low self-esteem, impatience, anger, frustration, and many other things can close off our receptivity to messages and also to our inner knowing. I find that I don't always recognize messages until it is too late to do anything about them. I list several examples of that later in this chapter.

15. In May 2003, one of our regular customers came into the shop looking for shirts for her two sons. As I attempted to concentrate on what she was saying I found I had to ask her to repeat things. I was so distracted that I finally had to interrupt her to tell her that I couldn't concentrate because I could feel the pain in her back. She said "Yes I have slipped a disc and am on my way to the doctor to get it put back in. My appointment is in ten minutes." I apologized and asked her if she would mind terribly if we chose the shirts after her appointment. She agreed and when she came back I had no trouble concentrating nor did she. With my empathic ability I don't feel the intensity of the physical pain of the other person; I actually feel the discomforts in the exact areas where the pain is and the distractions that the pain causes. I don't feel the distractions more intensely than the sufferer does but I am less used to living with it than they are so it seems to me to be intense.

16. Soon after that, in fact that same week, I had a telephone call from one of the other shop managers who is a personal friend of mine. As I spoke to her I had to lean on the wall because I had suddenly become very weak. I had to cut the call short because I began to slide down the wall while still completely conscious. I referred to this when in a channeling session at a later date and was told that I had given my friend my energy to help her through the operation she was having the next day. This was done on an unconscious level because I wasn't aware at that

stage that I could actually do that. I have since learnt just to stay open to allow healing energy to pass through me from source for others rather than deplete my own energy.

17. I had been working on my computer for a while and then I began to write a new article about a subject that had just come to me. It was getting late and I had written about a page when I felt I had reached a good place to stop. I had intended to resume writing the article at a later date but two days later I still hadn't managed to find the time. I sat down at the computer and thought I would just check my mail and visit a website I had intended to look at first before I resumed writing the article. On the website, posted that day, was a transcript of a channel that was (apart from a couple of words) the exact article I had begun to write two days earlier. The channel went on beyond what I had written of course. What happened? I have spoken to others about this and they have never heard of such a thing happening before. I can only speculate that either I was there energetically as part of the group and heard the channel or I had begun to download the same channeled words myself. I really have no idea and haven't thought to ask about this in our channel sessions. Needless to say I had to scrap the article. It brings up an interesting issue though. If we begin to be able to do that sort of thing more what happens to the laws concerning plagiarism.

18. After a channeling session with Caz as we were stretching and taking a break I heard a voice saying clearly – "They are going to put you on the table now." (When I say voice – there is no sound and yet I hear so clearly the message conveyed.) I assume that 'they' were Angel Addellesse my healing angel at that time and Angel Manayas my inspiration angel who had been speaking to me during our session and I again assume that whoever spoke to me must have been one of my guides at that time. It wasn't Caz and there wasn't anyone else in the house. I had taken my massage table with me this time to do the Reconnection for Caz and I guess spirit thought it a good opportunity to have Caz work on me with her Reiki skills as well.

All of the above are examples of occurrences which were coming with increasing regularity so I decided that I had no choice but to find out more about what was happening to me and how I might manage to live with it more successfully. Over the past year I hadn't been enjoying the work I was doing anyway so, in May 2003, the same month my divorce was finalized, I gave my employer three months notice planning to leave main stream work by the end of August. I became very busy with my personal life and chosen activities and of course things still happened. The following incidents are several examples of these.

1. *In 2004 I was still living in Oxley a suburb of Brisbane and had just driven back from Highfields just outside Toowoomba where I had been visiting friends for a few days. Instead of going straight home I decided to go to the local shopping centre to buy some fresh milk, etc. On my way home I was turning off Station Road into Englefield Road as a car was pulling away from the bowling club crossing a field where it would enter Englefield Road about 20 metres ahead of me. As I saw the man driving the car looking straight at me and slowing down to stop before reaching the road I heard in my head very calmly – "He's going to hit you". The man had stopped and was waiting so I said out loud in reply "don't be silly he's seen me". As I went by I had reached a speed of about thirty kilometres an hour when the other car suddenly shot out into the road. As I swerved into the right lane trying to get away from him I yelled "what are you doing?" The car kept coming and hit mine on the passenger side. I sat for a while bruised and stunned thinking "what the hell?" The warning probably came from Archangel Michael. I believed it to be a silly warning, so all I did as I passed the car was stay alert but didn't think quickly enough to ask Michael for help when the car shot towards mine. I had been warned by spirit that the way I would receive messages would be light and fleeting. I often wondered if the accident was deliberate but never thought to ask spirit about it until about three years later when I was at a festival and talking to my mother through an aura reader and she told me it was definitely unintentional.*

Why did I think the accident may have been deliberate? The driver of the car in his agitated state pulled an insurance form out of his glove box within a minute of the accident and presented it to me. This is a normal reaction for many after such a shock because it brings the agitated mind to bear on something they can control. While it seemed strange to me at the time it was definitely understandable but I was still dazed with my head resting on the steering wheel and thinking to myself "what the hell?"

2. *A year or so later I was returning to Queensland from a visit to northern New South Wales. Once I am on the road I usually do a long stretch without break or diversion from my course so, when I suddenly decided to turn off the highway and head for the north coast I thought "What are you doing? You haven't got time to go to the beach today". I turned around and got back on the highway heading home. A few minutes down the road I again turned off the highway, this time into an old 'road works' clearing. I stopped the car and walked the dog seeming to be in no hurry to resume my journey. Not understanding why I did this I got back in the car and continued my journey and about five minutes down the highway the traffic came to a dead halt and there we sat in Queensland's sweltering summer heat for about 20 minutes. I realized then that my guides were trying to spare me that discomfort. I had followed their urging twice but without any understanding at all therefore I continued on my way and fell into the situation that they were trying to help me avoid. I described this to spirit when speaking to them through Caz and asked if I was being deliberately diverted. The response was a very frustrated, "You are often being diverted Tarra. There are many times in your life when this has occurred."*

3. *In late 2007 I was traveling from Goonellabah in New South Wales to Highfields in Queensland which is a four and a half hour trip. I was just driving out of Lismore when it felt like my steering wheel had been grabbed by someone and pulled in short sharp very fast jerks - left right, left right, left right,*

left right. I knew it wasn't the car and said out loud, "but, I put new tyres on the front and had the wheels aligned and balanced and the car serviced? Everything's fine!" I kept driving and the steering wheel was pulled to the left toward the grassy verge. I straightened the wheel and kept driving saying again, "the car's fine". Sometimes you know we really do need to be hit over the head with a sledge hammer before we understand what is going on. I was right. There was absolutely nothing wrong with the car but in five minutes time there was something wrong with both the car and me. There was a stationary line of traffic on the bridge waiting to go through a small roundabout on the other side. We had been sitting there for a couple of minutes when I heard a crash, looked up and the front of my car was under the higher car in front of me. I was stunned and wondered why the car in front had backed into me. I couldn't work it out. No-one was really hurt, I had a slight tenderness in my chest from the seat belt but that was all. The others who observed what was happening said my car rolled under the other car and they asked if I fainted. I said I didn't think so.

After the formalities were done I was taken home by the tow truck driver and I called my brother to come down from Palm Beach and take me up to Highfields. I was going to a dear friend's funeral and really needed to be there. Three days later the funeral was over and I'd said goodbye to my friend. All of the visiting relatives had gone home and my chest was still sore so I went to have it x-rayed. The results showed that my sternum was fractured.

It occurred to me that there was no way that this could have happened if my hands were on the steering wheel and I wondered why they weren't. When I returned home I went to my GP explained what had happened and asked that I have a full medical examination done. Of course she told me I would need to be grounded while this was happening and yes of course I knew, bucking and screaming not withstanding, that she was right. So over the next three months numerous tests, x-rays, and brain scans were done. The results were back showing that everything was normal, blood pressure normal, no evidence of recent strokes. Finally I was sent to a specialist who explained a very common episode that people have. I was easily able to identify the triggers that would cause this reflex in me. These reflexes are mild for me and require a combination of at least three triggers to be present to knock me out for a second. Some triggers are high levels of stress, feeling ill or off-colour, heat, exhaust fumes, cleaning fluids, strong perfumes, and needles are just some of them. (For further information on this Google 'Vasovagal Syncope')

That day was particularly hot and I had my air vent on flow through with the fan on but the air conditioner off because we had been idling for quite a while and I didn't want the engine to overheat. Because of this I was hot, stressed, and breathing exhaust fumes (carbon monoxide) from the old car in front of me and the inevitable happened. I was given the all clear to drive again by the specialists however; I made some changes of my own. I now know to keep my air vent on circulate not flow through and to always have the air conditioner on cold even in winter.

I am telling you this whole story because of several things: -

The first is that I have fainted quite often when over-heated; stumbled and almost fallen when hit with a gust of fumes from industrial cleaners or very strong perfume and Doctors have done numerous test and everything is always normal. The second is that my guides were obviously trying to get a message across but I couldn't understand what was wrong. In fact, nothing was wrong they just wanted me to pull over and wait for the traffic hold-up to clear so that I wouldn't be exposed to the experience that occurred. The third is that I am grateful that I didn't because through that incident I finally found out why I had been passing out at odd times that seemed to have no identifiable pattern since I was ten years old.

The moral of these stories is to 'stay alert'. If you are being redirected or diverted, rather than ignore what is being shown, just trust that there is a good reason for it despite the fact that you don't understand the guidance.

CHAPTER 5

MY CONTINUING SEARCH

"I hear and I forget. I see and I remember. I do and I understand."

Confucius

Over the past two decades I have gone back to basics taking a four pronged approach from an untrained layman's perspective – religion, philosophy, social evolution, and spiritual development. I remembered the basics of Darwin's theory of evolution and also the 'Bible' so I didn't revisit those as I have done many in the past.

I began by reading 'How to Know God' by Deepak Chopra; 'Jesus The Man' by Barbara Thiering; 'Mysteries of Atlantis Revisited' by Edgar Evans Cayce, Gail Cayce Schwartzer, Douglas G Richards; and many other books of this nature besides. I looked into The Dreaming, and The Chinese Religion. Surprisingly I found it beneficial at this point to re-read two novels 'The Fountain Head' and 'Atlas Shrugged' by Ayn Rand.

Friends and family, seeing my interest, began giving me books that I love. My mother-in-law gave me the Reader's Digest 'Magic and Medicine of Plants' and my sister-in-law gave me my first pack of Angel Healing Cards and one of Doreen's books, 'The Lightworker's Way' by Doreen Virtue, Ph.D.

Enjoying the cards in particular, I purchased many other packs including Vernon Mahabal 's 'Palmistry Cards'; Dr Ronald L Bonewitz's 'Wisdom of the Maya; Jamie Sams & David Carson's 'Medicine Cards'; Ghao-Hsiu Chen's 'I Ching'; Leon Nacson's 'Dream Cards'; Toni Carmine Salerno's 'Crystal Oracle'; 'The Original Rider Waite Tarot'; and numerous packs of Doreen Virtues as well. I use all of these and find the tarot suits me best for in-depth readings. I also made my own runes during ceramic painting classes and consult them from time to time following the guidance of 'The Book of Runes' with commentary by Ralph Blum.

I began to buy and read more of Doreen's books and was drawn more and more to certain authors who wrote of the subjects I was interested in. I find these authors wonderful Deepak Chopra, Diana Cooper, John Edwards, Masaru Emoto, Louise Hay, Henneke Jennings, Shirley MacLaine, Thomas Moore, Caroline Myss, Dr. Eric Pearl, Carol S. Pearson, Jon Peniel, Sandy Stevenson, Tashira Tachiren, James Twyman, James Van Praagh, and Stuart Wilde. There are so many more I have read and so many more I haven't found the time to read.

I started reading about philosophers like Confucius, Nostradamus, Plato, *Pythagoras and Socrates. (*'The Life of Pythagoras' Collected and translated by M. Dacier. I found this 1981 reprint of the 1707 translation in 'Archives Fine Books' in Brisbane www.archives.com.au)

I intentionally saw documentaries on all sorts of subjects from natural healing remedies to space exploration; visited all sorts of web sites and books to learn of other people's experiences and journeys and how they had decided to live their lives as a result of those experiences. I read every channel by Lee Carroll, from first to last on www.kryon.com. What I was looking at more than anything was thought processes, reasoning processes, and how the individuals were interpreting those for themselves and then applying their conclusions to the way they live their lives.

On the heels of all of this then followed what I call spiritual-development overload. While still in the throes of this overload I spat the dummy and wrote the following article.

SPIRITUAL-DEVELOPMENT OVERLOAD

*"Don't be too timid and squeamish about your actions.
All life is an experiment. The more experiments you
make the better."*

Ralph Waldo Emerson

Yesterday I rebelled against God and the Universe; against all advice; against myself; and against reason. I didn't care about higher dimensions; higher vibrations; or good and bad. I just wanted oblivion. I have been to this place before at times and it does me harm, but you see, I don't care at the time. It is what I feel and what is happening to me, however . . . .

This time it suddenly occurred to me that I was on overload and a new consolidation and clearing was in progress. Now and again it would be wise for me to just go with the flow and trust my process. If I don't and if I don't recognize it for what it is then the inevitable happens and I am compelled to face my dark side. Unfortunately, quite often I don't recognize this early enough and have a few unpleasant hours of self-recrimination until my higher self regains control.

I had been reading about Pythagoras – his 'Life, Philosophy, Symbols and Verses'. At first I was awestruck and excited by his objectivity and astute understanding of a high moral code applicable to private and public matters. Then I became overwhelmed but still excited by the strict discipline one would need in order to live by that code.

I was also feeling quite petty yesterday worrying about me when throughout time Jesus and others around the world have been and are being persecuted despite their often blameless lives. Natural disasters are killing people around the globe right now and I'm worrying about me. It seems that all I am concerned about at this point is me. Only . . . that isn't quite true, I realize that my feeling of helplessness in these situations was contributing to my overload. I'm overwhelmed by the needs of people in distress. I send healing light around the world with the help of my family and friends throughout time and I know it is received. Still disasters occur.

As to the atrocities perpetrated on the innocent through war and terrorism in the guise of religion, individual and countries egos and pride, I feel like I'm being washed away in their blood and pain. This is where I go when I don't recognize overload. While I realize our world is healing itself by facing these hitherto unseen (by the general public to a large extent) atrocities and lifting the veil from our 'collective eyes', I also acknowledge that in the throes of my growing and healing pains I am contributing to the growth and healing of the 'Human Race's Collective Consciousness'. In that light, facing my dark side and working through what seems to be my petty problems becomes an extremely worthwhile exercise.

At times like these I feel quite alone and isolated. I feel that sharing this type of experience with others will help them to know that many people, more than may be thought, are walking similar paths of development. While ways of developing and growing spiritually may differ one is never really alone. We are always supported energetically.

If you've ever been where I have just described, you'll understand this part of my journey and the strength required to pull one's self out of it or to just surrender.

LEARNING AND RESEARCHING

In September 2003 I enrolled for Doreen Virtues 'Angel Intuitive Workshop'. During the workshop, apart from card readings, we were given exercises all of which I was pleasantly surprised to find I could do. The exercises involved partnering up with a different person each time.

1. *The first exercise was to hold my partners watch and then answer whatever question she asked. Her question was, "When will I meet my soul mate?" I closed my eyes and sat with the question for a while not expecting anything but to my surprise I saw myself standing in a garden at night. I could see through a window into a lighted bedroom and the girl was sitting on her bed reading. I realized this was what she always did at night and I was so surprised that I didn't stop to think. I said "You little devil you're not interested in meeting your soul*

mate. *In order to meet him you would need to go out." Her reply, "Sprung. I didn't have a question so I just made one up. I won't do that again!"*

2. *The second exercise was to read a persons aura. I walked to the back of the room and partnered with a woman in her early thirties who graciously let me read her. As we sat down and introduced ourselves I saw nothing around her. We smilingly began and when I focused in on her aura I was fascinated as I related what I saw. On her right were several men's faces, behind her and towering above her were huge figures that were quite wispy looking, at her left shoulder and down to her waist there were a number of smiling female faces and several children of different ages. Hovering in front of her at brow level was a full body profile of a chubby pink baby (it looked like the one in the old Michelin tyre ad). As we were called to move on to the next exercise a green, blue, and red parrot flew across in front of her at about chest height. I didn't get to tell her that until I saw her at lunch and had time to ask, "What did the parrot mean?" She replied, "I live where there are a lot of parrots."*

3. *After lunch we began the third exercise. We had over a hundred people to choose from so this time I moved down to the center of the right side of the room and found a lady of roughly my age who was willing to work with me. This time we were to focus on the colours in the person's auric field. While I sensed rather than saw colours they were overlaid with a grey smoky hue. As I sat telling her about her aura my throat and chest became constricted and I could barely breathe. I told her this and she explained, "Yes, I had a chest infection and am still recovering from it."*

4. *For the fourth exercise we were to do another aura reading so I moved further toward the front of the room and approached a lady that said I could work with her. As I looked into her aura I saw a gentleman. "There is a gentleman with grey hair and a very deeply lined face at your right shoulder. He is not that old he seems to be between forty-five and fifty." I scanned her aura*

further and said "I'm sorry, that's all I can see." She looked at me stony-faced and said "That's alright. I only wanted to know if my father was with me anyway." I didn't probe further. Some people are very open and easily read while others prefer to maintain their privacy and seem to be able to do this by closing themselves down. When I sense this I respect their wishes.

I had already done quite a bit of work with Doreen's Angel cards but the workshop rounded the knowledge off nicely for me and gave me new insights and a lot more confidence in my abilities. I am an Angel Intuitive and love to do those readings but get very little practice these days.

During the years 2004/2005 I continued to attend lectures, weekend courses and some workshops, observing or learning first hand from some interesting people like Artemis, Wayne Dwyer, Gypsy, Louise Hay, Caroline Myss, Julie and Peter O'Neill, Eric Pearl, Sandy Stevenson, and James Twyman.

I also went to watch James Van Praagh at work during a session at the Cultural Center in Brisbane. I was very impressed with the focus of his work that day when he connected with those passed over who had died tragic deaths, mostly suicides, which their loved ones in the audience were having difficulty coming to terms with. I watched the information they received lift heavy burdens from their shoulders. Every communication that day healed someone. Throughout the day while James was working there was a wonderful smell of burning incense. It was very calming and I wondered what it was called because I hadn't smelt that one before. During question time a member of the audience asked what incense he used. He explained that, for safety reasons, they weren't permitted to burn incense but audiences often ask about the scent used in his sessions.

It is my understanding that when we hold guilt about someone who has died or just can't let go of something to do with the manner of their death it makes it difficult for them to move on. We have laid many of my family members to rest over the past decade and I have learnt that grieving fully and resolving any issues I have concerning my relationship with them and then letting go if I can is a good thing for them and for me. I have found that I enjoy recalling the fond memories I hold of them and residual memories of any difficulties I encountered during our relationship fade over time.

In December, 2004 I attended Dr. Eric Pearls Seminars that he presented in Sydney and after doing Levels I & II & III became a 'Reconnection Practitioner'. Eric developed a modality that is very effective in assisting the individual to heal and he has some wondrous stories to tell. I won't go into the details here but if you wish to learn more about his experiences and his work his book is interesting, self-explanatory, and a fast read. It is Dr. Eric Pearl 'The Reconnection'. After qualifying as a practitioner I began my practice in Brisbane.

I attended an interesting one day Seminar in Brisbane given by Caroline Myss about her work on energy medicine and human consciousness. Her book 'ANATOMY OF THE SPIRIT' is very powerful. I am also interested in her views on self-esteem. She has produced a 4 x tape audio that is well worth listening to if low self-esteem is an issue for you. It is 'SELF-ESTEEM' Your Fundamental Power by Caroline Myss.

CHAPTER 6

COMMITTING TO
MY LIFES FOCUS

*"We live in a moment where change is so speeded up
that we begin to see the present only when it is already
disappearing."*

R. D. Laing

The three months notice I had given my employer finished at the end of
August 2003 and I was finally free to begin planning my new life.

Having taken the steps to consciously change careers and commit to my
beliefs, I also wanted to make a few more personal changes. I wanted to
move from Brisbane to north eastern New South Wales; sell off property;
buy a new car because I was planning to do a lot of traveling; and I wanted
to change my name. Our divorce had already come through in May 2003
but I put off changing my name then and planned to do it when I moved
so that it could be done along with all of the paperwork involved in moving
inter-state. I'm far from fond of paperwork these days.

So first things first, I cleared out everything I felt I no longer needed and
gave it away. It seemed to take forever to go through all of the paperwork
that remained from our thirty-nine year relationship, interests, respective
careers, and three businesses. Finally this was done and sensitive paperwork
safely destroyed.

Mid-way through 2004 I began the hard work of preparing my house for sale by removing wallpaper and carpet; repairing, sanding and painting walls; and repairing and painting cupboards inside and out. Establishing bigger gardens; having the house, landing and railings repaired where needed and then painted; the roof tiles repaired or replaced where needed then cleaned. All of that took me until early 2006. I did the garden and inside work myself except for the final touches of resealing the shower recess and polishing the floors. It was also necessary for me to employ a painter to do the eaves and main body of the outside of the house because it was high-set and a bit too difficult for me to reach.

At this time, because of the bush fires down south, tradesmen were difficult to find for the small jobs I needed done. Two of my brothers, Graham and Tim, came to the rescue with leveling the house and repairing the back landing, patio, railings and steps which were jobs that I didn't have the expertise to do. My house went on the market mid 2006, and after a false sale and three unsupportable offers, it finally sold in early September 2006.

Between selling my old home and moving into my new one, which was about six weeks, my youngest brother Tim graciously allowed me to make my home with him. When we were ready he and Graham moved me from Brisbane to Goonellabah, a part of Lismore in New South Wales. I had the pleasure of the company of Tim and my nieces, Rhiannon (4) and Hermione (3) for almost two months while we settled me into my new home and I felt blessed to be in their company. Tim also did the repairs that were needed and built a fence for my dog Saanu and other necessary jobs.

Sadly while all of this was going on my mother died and one of her brothers and one of her sisters, my Uncle Leslie and Aunty Heather also passed away. My sister Heather had a tumor removed near her pineal gland. My dear sister-in-law Sinimoa lost her battle with cancer and left us too. These were very emotional times for the whole family. There were some happy times too when Sinimoa and Graham's eldest son Peter and his partner Kylie gave birth to their first child and later when everything settled down they were married. We were all still a little emotionally raw so there were tears of happiness at the wedding mixed with tears of sadness that Sinimoa couldn't be there in person. She was there though because I saw her; she was wearing her pink suit and standing at Peter's left shoulder listening intently as they made their wedding vows.

Still, life goes on and the emotional roller coaster ride we had all been on over the past few years through the sad and happy times helped all of our family to learn more about ourselves and what was important to us.

I think all of the things that my brothers were helping me with at that time help us all to cope with the losses, dazed though we may have been.

CHAPTER 7

COMING TO TERMS WITH LOSS

"Life does not cease to be funny when people die any more than it ceases to be serious when people laugh."

George Bernard Shaw

As we reach our fifties we notice that many of our Aunts and Uncles; some of our cousins, friends and in-laws; and even aged pets begin to depart this life with increasing regularity. We seem to be visiting hospitals and family to offer support and comfort to them as well as seeking it for ourselves. For several years my family was saying goodbye to so many loved ones. These events throw our emotions all over the place. They are generally heightened to such a degree that something remotely sad will see us sobbing uncontrollably and the least bit funny will have us roaring with laughter. Reacting naturally to our emotions as they come up is a very healthy way of dealing with stress. Emotional honesty releases the tension created by stress and keeps us balanced and centered. Many do this openly and in the moment and others, like me, wait until they are alone before releasing all that they have pent up.

1. When my father-in-law was dying the family received a call warning us that his time was near. It was 3:00 am and I dressed in the dark not wanting to wake the household. My

sister-in-law and I arrived at the car park at the same time. We were walking across to the main hospital building when I happened to look down at my feet. There was I, perfectly made-up and dressed in a yellow winter suit with black top and accessories, sporting a plain black leather court shoe on one foot while on the other I wore a black suede court shoe with a bow. When I stopped short my sister-in-law noticed too and we both laughed heartily fueled by tension and stress.

2. We were standing with my mother-in-law at her brother's graveside, while the minister was saying the words committing his body to the ground, when suddenly a rather large goanna ran up one of the men's trouser legs. The whole group tried not to laugh at the man's antics as he freed himself of the creature. We subdued our laughter, wearing suitable expressions as soon as we could – some succeeded, others didn't. The deed however, was done and a lot of tension was released from the mourners. Later, my very proper mother-in-law smiled and said that we had been too serious and her brother really wouldn't have liked that.

3. I was crying, actually sobbing; feeling sick to the stomach and mourning the death of someone who I was very close to. Suddenly I was outside of myself observing my pain and saying "this is not real." Still sobbing I felt my soul-self say *"she is going home"* while my emotional and physical-self were feeling the pain of her parting. Both were so real to me at that point and while the pain didn't lessen over the next few months, because there were issues to resolve in my psyche about our relationship, somehow my soul-self helped my human-self through the mourning process. Anger, regret, love, fond memories, bad memories, resentments, gratitude all came up to be dealt with in record time. Sometimes the experience is quite different and while thinking about this latest loss not too kindly I heard *"Everyone is doing the best that they can"*. I was working at my computer at the time and found myself pounding my mouse down on my desk and saying "Well it just isn't good enough." A very complex process, for you see,

I was saying goodbye to my mother. When Mum died I felt a huge void. Not the one you feel when someone close to you has died for I have said goodbye to many a family member before. The void I felt was palpable. I physically felt the edge of the cliff with my feet as I stood looking out into the mist of nothingness. The only thing that stopped me from falling was the strong pressure I felt pushing me back holding me teetering on the edge. Still I felt like I might fall. There was a massive energy connection from source that my Mother anchored here on earth. I had no idea of the type of energy she held for her family until she and it were no longer there. I had never felt that before not even when my father and grandparents died. Perhaps it was because I was not consciously working with the energies back then. Mum loved nature and, like all of us and through us, connected heaven to earth. I wonder if this was it or was it the connection that the oldest daughter has with her mother. I do not know but I am pleased that I experienced what I did, painful as it was at the time. It was a sudden shock to find myself energetically standing at the edge of that cliff and hearing the words. *"Step up. It's your turn now."* I didn't understand fully what was meant by that at the time, but I believe I do now. This energy was a stabilizing or buffering one and not one I was consciously used to dealing with. I was more used to a fluctuating energy and so the change was easily felt. I soon filled the void with my own energy and instinctively felt that it was my generations turn to hold the energy for the family. There are so many levels we work on and one of them is with our earth family on both sides of the veil. As I said earlier life goes on so I had a shower, dressed, made my self up as best as my puffy eyes would allow and went across the highway to buy a new mouse to replace the one I had just pulverized.

4. When one of my friends died, I went to stay with his wife, also a dear friend, to support her in preparing for his funeral and to honour him by celebrating his life here on earth. All who have lived and die deserve that from us. This dear friend

was ninety-one years old and right up to the days before his death never stopped learning and insisting that he was able to do things for himself. His wife and I both learnt so much about living a full life from him and also our view of aging and life expectancy is quite different from what many believe. Where others may view their late seventies as old and failing we know for a certainty that we can expect to be active and sprightly into our late eighties and beyond if we wish it to be so and even if we wish it not to be so. All of the arrangements for the funeral had been made and a group of us were sitting around the kitchen table after dinner. We were roaring with laughter at the jokes being read out loud by my friend's son for all to hear. Passing the book around we continued to read out jokes for quite a while. We were exhausted by the time we went to bed which was exactly what we needed to ensure we at least rested even if we couldn't sleep. Later in the privacy of my room there were tears. They were healing tears that were relieving tension and stress.

CHAPTER 8

STREAMLINING MY LIFE

"Dance as though no one is watching. Love as though you have never been hurt. Sing as though no one can hear you. Live as though heaven is on earth."

Souza

The path to ascension is the spiritual thread running through my life. I have been all the things many of us have been throughout our life experiences. Some of those have even repeated themselves in this life. I, like many others, have a low self-esteem issue to overcome. Feelings of this still remain but they are only habits and shadows. They are illusions however their imprint on my psyche is tenacious.

(I will not give you surnames here to respect the families' privacy.) At my birth my parents named me Margaret Joan and with my surname in numerology was a 3. Without its powerful vibration I may not have been able to face the challenges of my childhood. I have not included those experiences in this book wanting its focus to be placed squarely on my spiritual development.

When we married, I took Keith's surname my name in numerology then was a 2. Obviously, having read my book this far, you already know that my focus is not placed on this experience either. We shared a total of thirty-nine years during our relationship and learnt a lot from each other. Was it a mistake? No. Our relationship ran its course until it was just time to move on. He recognized this and took his leave. Was the parting amicable? Yes. It was however, emotionally challenging despite the fact that it was time. I don't believe we can have a long standing relationship of any sort without feeling the ties being severed and the drifting that comes after it.

During my adult life I have often used the name 'Jo' or 'Tarra' when signing what I have written; I like both names much better than the ones my parents gave me. Jo is present in Joan and Tarra is formed out of Margaret. After our divorce I had the opportunity to use my maiden name or follow my heart. I chose my heart and decided that I wanted to work with a new vibration and chose a name that I liked to support me in achieving that end. It is one that I have used since 2002.

I changed my name by deed poll and became Tarra (22) Logan (22) = (44) = (8). I am not well versed in numerology; I haven't yet taken the time to study it. Tarra is pronounced exactly the same as Tara. Logan, which just happens to hold the right vibration, is my great-grandparents surname through the female line.

With this change I wanted to bring balance to my life along with ending the wallowing in old karmic energy already cleared; get on with the business of becoming all that I can be, hopefully, by slowing down my ascension process to a more manageable pace.

So I sold my old house in Queensland and bought my new house in my new legal name of Tarra Logan in New South Wales. The Real Estate Agents in both states didn't even bat an eyelid and just worked through the changes with me. They were great! Moving interstate requires a lot of paperwork changes at the best of times but with my change of name too I had to keep a check list for a few months to ensure everything was done correctly.

I am now snuggly settled into my new life and new home in the hills of Goonellabah. My house backs onto forty acres of privately owned land not yet developed which has become a nature corridor for the local wildlife. I have so many different birds to watch, many large lizards some snakes of course, bush turkeys, wallabies, and koalas. The old male koala comes and nestles in the tree on my back terrace and often spends a whole day there during the winter months. My house is two stories high at the back so I can watch him almost eye to eye – its absolute heaven.

Now you may wonder why I told you about my name change at all. It is because I am presenting transcripts of channels verbatim and during them the same entity sometimes addressed me using Margaret and Tarra interchangeably. For simplicity and clarity I use Tarra only. The only other changes I make to the transcribed channels is when I omit information personal to another or add a word to clarify a point made and those changes are bracketed.

PART TWO

CHAPTER 9

MY TAKE ON CHANNELING

There are a couple of interesting points to note about the way spirit communicates with us.

The first is that they tailor their conversation to their audience, mostly using the scope of language common to both the channeler and the recipients. It would be of no benefit to me or Caz for them to speak to us as they would a room full of Doctors or Scientists. What would be the point in that? These are tailored specifically for me although they, more than I, would know of the probability of me transcribing them for others to read.

Sometimes the person channeling may not be familiar with specific scientific language but is nevertheless familiar with the technical words necessary to bring forward a technical communication if that is what some in the audience need to hear. For example, Kryon brings forward concepts difficult for Lee Carol to express to a mixed audience at times and therefore before doing so he warns and advises Lee to "go slowly my partner" to ensure accuracy.

The other interesting thing that we need to be aware of is that, while we are communicating with 'spirit', entities on the other side are also listening to what is being said and are curious about our reactions to it. They are very excited now as our growth quickens. So, when we are in channel sessions many come to listen to us; to learn from us; and to observe us with love. We have a big audience when we are open to channel because in opening up to channel we have invited open communication with the light. Those who know us personally are as eager as we are to communicate and miss us even more than we do them. Why is that? I think it is because, unlike us who don't always know that they exist, they known that we exist and they love us. I have heard of their presence in other channeled messages and have evidence of this in my own awareness of them and also in the channeled message from Mars dated 5th December, 2005.

Almost all of our communications in the following transcripts deal mainly with my personal struggles and growth. 'The team' knows that I like to be teased, albeit lovingly, and they almost always deliver which is fabulous fun. They also know that I will not be shy or embarrassed, in the most part, to ask silly questions or put forward my own way of seeing things. They know too, that I like to have my channels come through as conversations and not lectures; that I have a short attention span; and that I tie the most surprising and seemingly impossible concepts together quite often.

When we are in open session like this with spirit there is no possibility of hiding my true thoughts. Generally though, they don't pull me up on these things because, I believe, they like me to have the realizations for myself first before they broach the subject. They are Masters of validation once I admit to things and I find that after an insight has occurred validation is usually presented to me immediately or within days while the insight is still fresh in my mind.

Lastly, I believe the quality of the information received is often determined by the questions asked. If I don't word the questions right (I often struggle with this) or delve deeper with a further question it can be an opportunity missed. At other times the questions being answered are ones I have put to spirit during the days and weeks leading up to the channeling session.

INTRODUCING CAZ

Throughout my journey I have accumulated tapes from all different sessions from Tarot readings to channeled messages, usually from the 'Mind, Body, Spirit Festivals' I went to in Brisbane and Sydney and the country one that is on twice a year in Toowoomba. I've also experienced having my aura read, my astrology chart done, and received messages through a lovely lady in Brisbane who does automatic writing. A while ago, I had a very strong urge that would not be denied, to arrange a telephone session with Kerrie O'Connor, a world renowned Clairvoyant Master and Intuitive Teacher in the US. When my sweet little old dog Saanu was dying I contacted Amanda De Warren who lives here in Ipswich, Queensland. www.amandadewarrenpets.com . Amanda communicates with our pets here and with those that have passed over. The interesting thing is that those pets bring through people that they were close to; those that we may otherwise not have contact with. They have a very strong connection to us and the veil we often find difficult to penetrate seems to be nothing for them.

I have chosen to use transcripts from only one of these wonderful people for this book and they are those channeled through Caz Greene. The first of my reasons for doing this is because messages I have received from others have been confirmed during Caz's sessions and vice versa and the second is that we were also able to maintain continuity for two years with the work we were doing with spirit.

Caz's website is www.cazheartlight.com ; she specializes in past life journeys and many people around the world avail themselves of her expertise. After reading the transcripts from the audio tapes of my sessions with her, I think you will agree with me that Caz's specialty encompasses much more than that as the information on her website also attests. Although I commissioned these sessions and the tapes are mine, they are Caz's work too so, I thought it necessary to ask her permission before presenting them here and she bravely and graciously agreed.

It would not surprise you to know that Caz was the lady I was able to read so clearly during Doreen Virtues' Workshop because her energy field is so clear and open. That is where we first met and over the past twelve years I have treasured her as a dear friend. She is the only one I know personally who does trance channeling but I am aware that there are many others here in Australia and of course around the world.

Basically Caz is overshadowed by the spirit communicating through her and when this is done I can see the entity or a scene in my minds eye quite often. When the channel is over it is a little like a dream for Caz in that she remembers some of what has occurred for a short time only. After that it is then necessary for me to remind her of what was said if I refer back to channels in conversation with her at a later date. She finds this to be a little frustrating to handle at times.

When we first began doing these sessions, a couple of times when Caz popped back in wanting to answer the question herself, the connections were broken. Caz, like me, likes to be involved in conversations with her friends and to speculate on and discuss issues. It is like bread and butter to us or these days more like a good Caesar Salad. That is why I trust the messages coming through and why I am comfortable with them being filtered through Caz's personal method of communication.

A large portion of my process is reflected in the questions I ask of 'spirit' through channel. The questions themselves tell me a lot about my relationship to 'self' while the answers to my questions provide me with insights into my relationship to all things. Throughout these dialogues there were opportunities for me to delve deeper by asking more personal questions. I rarely did that because I wasn't sure I would be strong enough to face the answers. Anyone interested in past lives for example would realize that theirs could be many and varied; from beggar to Queen or King; the murderous to the pious; open minded to closed; courageous to fearful; gentle to violent; etc. Personally, I am certain that I do not want to remember all of them now unless the memories are capable of serving me in some way in this life or with my path toward ascension. It is enough to know that the etheric archaisic records and the archaisic records in the cells of my body carry the wisdom gained from those experiences. The personality of my soul is the one area I haven't explored closely yet however, through some of the comments made by 'The Team' I have gained some insights into my souls core character.

I believe that there is information in these channels which, while personal to me, may be useful to many others around the world. If we are 'one' contributing to and exposed to the same energy then there is no way that we can escape being affected by that energy to a certain degree.

These higher level entities (for want of a better definition) who come through respect and love us unconditionally and will only respond to our requests. If in a channel you are being judged, blamed, or criticized my advice is to sever the contact immediately for it is likely that you are not communicating with an entity of the light. My initial call to spirit was to ask that I learn the truth and that is what I perceive them to be giving me while what they are really doing is 'loving me'. That is all there is really. To understand this better go to www.ahashouse.com and close your eyes and listen to the video clip on his home page. You can also experience Aha's energy while Nicole interviews him on the News for the Soul website.

From my human perspective the only real truth that I perceive is that we create our own existence and what we draw to us is what we need to learn. They are our lessons so, from what I have gathered so far, energy is and that is all there is and where we perceive differences is the energy always bringing itself into balance. One particle vibrating extremely fast creating the illusion of innumerable particles and waves interacting when it is in fact one interacting and learning about it's 'self'. That is what some say. Others say that the one particle split into many and because they are parts of 'them self' they are always energetically connected – they are one. What I am trying to say here I think is that, as we learn and begin to understand more, the knowledge increases the light we hold within us and in turn that light lifts us up into heightened awareness.

CHAPTER 10

TRANSCRIPTS OF CHANNELS

"We often hear only what is being said rather than listen to all that is being communicated."

Anon

I am actually enjoying reviewing the tapes to see what ones would be suitable to include. All would be of course and obviously you can choose which ones you read. I would like to suggest though that initially, they be read by session date to keep the messages in context.

At the time these channels were done I had no idea that I would be writing about them so the first channels that we did and a couple of others weren't taped. Information from them is referred to in later channels however the clarity of those subsequent channels remains in tact.

While the transcript from the tapes is clear and certain the hesitancy you see at the beginning of the Imhotep channel for example comes from it being unclear to me. When Caz goes into her trance channel I go part way with her and it takes me a little longer for the connection to stabilize.

I just have to tell you too that during the channeling there is a lot of information being imparted and a lot of laughter and fun being had by all of us. While this is going on there is also healing being done for both Caz and I. Other activations are being done for us particularly by Jesus

Christ the Master Healer. Always, in the weeks following these sessions, any personal issues that I needed to work on would be highlighted for my attention and inevitable clearing.

6 September, 2004

COUNCIL OF PLEIADES

Caz: - "................OK............"

Pleiadians: - "We are here and we are from Pleiades and this is why you brought this tape today. We are aware that you have questions that you'd like to ask. We are here to answer them to the best of our ability. You may start as you wish."

Tarra: - "Well, to do with Pleiades, I'm not sure. But . . . I went to a Kinesiologist the other day and she claims I'm holding a secret to epilepsy in my solar plexus and that's what's causing so much agony for me. And . . . I don't know whether that's the sort of question I need to ask you or not. Also my throat is sore, but she also said some things like . . . um . . . there are two entities attached to me and I'm not sure that's right. So can you put some light on that?"

Pleiadians: - "Yes. There is a key held within your solar plexus. All you need to do is simply turn and unlock this key; this will let the energy flow outward and you will get messages and instincts for things to do for follow-up from this. As to the two entities, you have one on either shoulder. These are curious entities who are wanting . . . to see where you are going to go next."

Tarra: - "And . . . they are not a problem for me?"

Pleiadians: - "They are not causing any harm but it would be best to shake them off. Archangel Michael will assist you with this. They are

just along for the ride and you don't need your energy depleted any further."

Tarra: - "No. Thank you."

Pleiadians: - *"As to the epilepsy, this was also a past life thing where you were a child with epilepsy who was shunned. Turning this key will help release this from your energy – from your aura. Don't . . . we don't want you to stress too much in terms of this because it will come naturally and easily when the time is right. Many things happen on the energy levels that you are not aware of. You concern yourself too much with bringing them into the physical, into the now, when in truth for them to remain in the spiritual and energy levels is better."*

Tarra: - "So, I don't need to off-load that information somewhere? Put it down somewhere – it won't cause me any more pain?"

Pleiadians: - *"It won't cause you any more pain, you simply need to turn the key and it will release it into the energy levels and those who need to get this energy as messages will get them."*

Tarra: - "OK. I just read a book ("What is Lightbody?") by Archangel Ariel or channeled by Archangel Ariel (through Tashira Tachi-ren) and I'm not sure I understand it completely. Is it from 9th dimension, and . . . ?"

Pleiadians: - *"You are correct it is from 9th and 10th dimension and this book is correct and truth as we know it; as you will experience it. Again, this is something that you are experiencing more on the spiritual levels than the physical. Don't strain your human brain, and we do not mean any offence by this, don't strain the human brain to understand – let the words be absorbed into your psyche and they will be understood on those levels."*

Tarra: - "I'm not offended by that. I understand that I know things at different levels. So does that mean I've just gone into that 9th dimension and 10th dimension type level because it's seems a little different?"

Pleiadians: - "You often work on these levels."

Tarra: - "Right . . . ."

Pleiadians: - "You often work on these levels as you are sleeping and sometimes you will find that during the day you will have moments where . . . it's not to say that you black out, but you . . . another phrase would be zone out for a moment and you sort of shake yourself and come back. You have traveled to those dimensions. You are simultaneously working on five dimensions at the moment, even as you go about your daily business."

Tarra: - "Oh. I'm pleased I'm being useful somewhere."

Pleiadians: - "Indeed (sounding amused), this is so."

Tarra: - "If feels . . . it feels in this human life, like I'm not achieving very much. I don't mean that in a negative way; it just seems like I'm not moving as others expect me to move – naturally. The Kinesiologist also asked why I wasn't writing."

Pleiadians: - "Yes. We are very satisfied with your progress and we think you should be more satisfied with yourself as well; particularly . . . the difficulty for humans is in not realizing that they are a multi-dimensional being working on all these other dimensions. Most emphasis is put in the physical in the human world. So, it is difficult to clarify the experience you have and the abilities you have in the physical when the majority of this is being worked through in the spiritual levels and dimensions. Yes, the writing is an important thing which will come slowly as you write down your experiences and your feelings. But . . . you have done this before in other lives, when you were a scribe in Egypt and also in Greece. So these are natural things for you to do, which is why the Kinesiologist was concerned as to why you were not doing it now because she could see these energies around you. Ah . . . to a certain extent confusing them with your past lives as Kinesiologist are picking up energies that you are carrying with you from these times however don't push yourself. Things will come as they need to and if your psyche decides that this is something you need to experience in this life, you will."

Tarra: - "Right . . . I . . . um . . . I haven't been . . . I've been wondering why I wasn't doing it. And, actually I've been wondering why I pull back when I learn more? I have a tendency to pull back from things like affirmations, meditations, sending out light. Why am I pulling back?"

Pleiadians: - "This is a physical thing. It has been difficult for you to wrap your brain around the fact that you are multi-dimensional and that you do not have the physical limitations that you have trained yourself to believe. Um . . . this is why particular affirmations are very, very powerful but it really takes quite a bit of work and understanding for the human mind to accept that words, intentions and feelings can change the physical. When we so often see you experiencing physical difficulties and your emotions and feelings and thoughts seem to come after the physical feelings, to your perceptions. As in . . . ah, to clarify . . . your language . . . um . . . for instance (you) think you're feeling that pain is coming from a stomach cramp, when in fact the pain is to warn that there is a stomach problem that needs to be dealt with and will get worse if not dealt with . . . as opposed to it being so chronically bad that the pain is the last signal; the last warning. It is in fact the other way around."

Tarra: - "It's the first warning?"

Pleiadians: - "Yes."

(A portion omitted here. I take a holistic approach to health so am interested in what the Pleiadians have to say.)

Tarra: - "Um . . . my memory's difficult."

Pleiadians: - "That's fine, we have time."

Tarra: - "Oh. The Kinesiologist also asked why I was preventing or resisting her clearing . . . um . . . tension or something from my legs. That's not the first time this has been mentioned when I have had massages they've said to me "relax your legs" but to me, they seem to be relaxed."

Pleiadians: - "This is very much because of your control issues. This is where you feel it is a weakness to give up yourself to others. It is also to you a weakness to be stationary, which is why it is manifesting itself in your legs because the legs are the physical component for moving us forward. And, you are reluctant for others to move you forward without your permission. Even though you are giving your permission at these times it has been so ingrained in you that it is showing itself on the energetic levels."

Tarra: - "Right . . ."

Pleiadians: - "Again, this is something that you can stop by realizing that these people who you have come to or are drawn to, are also drawn to you on the spiritual levels to do this work."

Tarra: - "Thank you. She also saw a string of beings, hands together, going out from my right side. Are they the ones, like when I call in people to use my white light around the world; are they the ones I called in?"

Pleiadians: - "Yes, that is so. It is also a symbol to show you that we, from Pleiades are with you, your family throughout time. You'll find that your soul group of those around the world, working with the white light and other light, are generally from the Pleiades star system, for you."

Tarra: - "Right . . ."

Pleiadians: - "This is not to say that all those around the world are from the Pleiades star system, Caz for instance her group is from Orion."

Tarra: - "Ah. Do we get on well with them then?" (Laughter)

Pleiadians: - "At this time, yes. All star systems have had their growth."

Tarra: - "So it's not like, when I've called someone in like that it's not necessary to break it – break that connection?"

Pleiadians: - "No. In fact it would not be broken."

Tarra: - "(The Kinesiologist) she was concerned that I called in these entities that I have on my shoulders. I don't recall doing that?"

Pleiadians: - "You did, indeed. It is simply, in your request for higher knowledge and higher learning, there have been times when you have not been as guarded as you should. That is not to say you have to wear heavy protection but there are some who have higher knowledge but still carry with it ego."

Tarra: - "Right . . ."

Pleiadians: - ". . . And these entities that have come to you are like that. They want to impart their knowledge and have you do their bidding but they have no influence over you without your further permission."

Tarra: - "I have felt that, they have been . . . even though I'm having a struggle with ego a little bit . . . . . . I have felt that they have been manipulating that."

Pleiadians: - "Yes, indeed. That is why the sooner that you seek Archangel Michael the better. They are holding on very tentatively because of most of the work that you have been doing over time. They have very little purchase on you. A year ago it was stronger."

Tarra: - "So they have been with me for quite a while?"

Pleiadians: - "Yes, yes . . . ."

Tarra: - "I've actually noticed though . . . in the last few weeks, that it isn't me that's doing the ego thinking and the depression thing."

Pleiadians: - "Yes, that's right."

Tarra: - "Um, it's been different."

Pleiadians: - *"You're able to shrug them off like an old coat that you no longer need to wear They have no recourse of action in this."*

Tarra: - "No. So, in protecting . . . . I'm not quite sure I understand for example with my little friend when she had three spirits attached to her . . . are they called spirits?"

Pleiadians: - *"They're . . . they're an energy . . . I mean a spirit. A spirit is generally a manifestation of that soul still attached to that particular life, whereas an entity is the soul in a form that contains many energies from many different lives. It's hard to express it in the human (language)."*

Tarra: - "Yes anyway, so, I'm sort of surprised that if my energy can help the entities leave my friend, why it can't move these entities from me?"

Pleiadians: - *"It certainly can. You have the protection and strength however, of Archangel Michael behind you as well. Remember you are always a very strong channel for Archangel Michael in particular. There is no reason for instance, to shift a hill of dirt by your self when others are offering to help."*

Tarra: - "No."

Pleiadians: - *"Others with greater strength; it's OK to accept help. Does it make you a weaker person? It means you can conserve your energy for other things."*

Tarra: - "OK."

Pleiadians: - *"These entities have not been harmful in a great way. In fact there have been times when the information they have imparted has been quite helpful. But, at other times it has caused nothing but confusion; trying to fill your head with information that is not quite right for you and not for your energy."*

Tarra: - "No. I still . . . . I think I still keep my focus on where I'm going despite it, but it has been difficult."

Pleiadians: - *"Yes. It is like trying to climb a hill with a sodden back pack full of rocks."*

Tarra: - "Yes, I'm not sure what else I need to ask. I might think of some things later on. Is there any more information you wish to give me?"

Pleiadians: - *"There is. We're letting you know that Lord Ashtar is still watching over you."*

Tarra: - "Lovely."

Pleiadians: - *"And he asks that you, if you have not already done it, that you keep a journal beside your bed because he has been taking you on small journeys already. He says you are in extremely deep dream state during this time otherwise it would have caused physical problems for you and . . . not to worry if you cannot recall this. Just to accept that you are doing great, great works on his behalf and as a human we understand the great curiosity that we do not have. That you would like to know and to experience all these things in the physical as well but that you are not capable . . . . . your physical body is not capable of accepting these levels of energy . . . . . ah, without great calamity."*

Tarra: - "So, there's not even an instance where I can remember that?"

Pleiadians: - *"There may be memories because you are a very strong and powerful person but do not try to bring that full energy into your physical body but to keep that mantle of light protection around you. This is not to block; it's to protect your physical body because people make themselves quite ill* (If they don't do this). ***There are instances of humans putting themselves into situations of having to go into mental facilities through a blow-out of energies. So it is important to accept that many things happen on many different multi-dimensional levels that you do not need to bring into the physical."***

Tarra: - "No. I am a little bit disappointed and confused about why I can't talk to you myself? I love using Caz and being with Caz but I'm a bit confused why I can't connect and other people seem to be able to connect?"

Pleiadians: - "This is a blockage that you have created for yourself. Deep inside you, you have a self-esteem problem that still remains where you still put others higher than yourself forgetting you are an extremely wise being of many, many, many infinite lives. You need to drop your guard and to relax and to trust more. When you . . . you strain too hard. It will come when you accept you have this."

Tarra: - "Yes, yes. I thought it might be because I don't have enough information yet?"

Pleiadians: - "No. This is exactly the reason why you are having difficulties because you thought you didn't have enough information yet; you thought you weren't good enough yet. These thoughts are blocking you and, if you are willing to, affirmations will help this over time. You need to be more patient with yourself and to accept yourself like a tiny child. Just to explain, you need to nurture yourself as that tiny child who is just learning, but has infinite potential."

Tarra; - "Mmm . . ."

Pleiadians: - "You may speak."

Tarra: - "I've forgotten . . . I've forgotten what I was going to ask. (Laughter) Oh! My sister-in-law . . . . . when I was at the hospital one time, she said she saw me cloaked in a sheet and there was a black head coming at my head and sort of slanting off because it couldn't penetrate the sheet. Did she actually see that?"

Pleiadians: - "Yes. This . . . she saw you on another level. This is how we perceive you – a shining white being who is well protected from the majority of other entities."

Tarra: - "Right, OK . . ."

Pleiadians: - "What she saw was simply to let her know that is who you are and that you are not one who attracts dark entities to attach to yourself. The two . . . I need to emphasize; the two ones attached to you are not dark entities."

Tarra: - "No."

Pleiadians: - "They simply do not need to be there."

Tarra: - "Yes, well they're mischievous."

Pleiadians: - "That's right."

Tarra: - "I was given a book title. I can't remember what the book title is but it talks about a planet that's in the dark; lives in the dark and is near earth at the moment . . . and is trying to draw earth to it or it to earth into the light. And the entities from that cause mischief. Is that true?"

Pleiadians: - "Yes it is present on one level but it is still a lower level. Most of us are on a higher level than this and this has no interference for us. It can only cause mischief for those of the lowest levels."

Tarra: - "OK, so the book is worth reading then?"

Pleiadians: - "Yes, it's worth reading but we advise not to fill your mind and body with the energy of this because that is where the harm comes in from bringing in fear."

Tarra: - "Yes. I have a book at the moment by Stuart Wilde. I'm a bit concerned whether I should bother to read it or not because I don't feel I need to challenge my beliefs. Um, I'm sorry I can't remember the name of it; it's on my cupboard at home; black cover, I think its God's . . . some sort of fighting force or angel force. (The book is 'God's Gladiators' by Stuart Wilde and I loved it! My friend did not.)

Pleiadians: - "We have great affection for Stuart Wilde; we love his irreverent manner. It is worth reading."

Tarra: - "Thank you. I cannot recall any other questions at the moment."

Pleiadians: - *"That is fine. We have the fairies who are here who are coming in now. We must take our leave; they wish to speak to you."*

THE FAIRIES

Tarra: - "Oh! Hello, what would you like to tell me? (A bit nervously because I haven't spoken to fairies before and wasn't sure I believed in them.)"

Fairies: - *"We are so grateful that you have come here today to play with us. We want to lead you by your hand; take you out in nature; have you feel and experience the air and the energies around you and to accept our healing."* (Their communication is light and fast.)

Tarra: - "Thank you; I'll be very happy to. Do you see me at home when I am in the garden?"

Fairies: - *"Yes, particularly in the garden and we often see you through the windows. Some of us venture in closer but the energy of inside houses can bring us down quite quickly. Its density is not what we are used to so in houses we are always drawn to flowers and to brightly coloured things and to wind chimes which we adore."*

Tarra: - "Ah, I love wind chimes but I don't have flowers in my house. I don't (often) have flowers."

Fairies: - *"We know that many people are afraid to cut flowers because they feel it is taking away the energy from the earth. And we instead say the flowers are a joyful sacrifice that would like to come in and bring their beauty into your home."*

Tarra: - "And if I brought flowers into my home would you be able to come in near them?"

Fairies: - "We will come in more often. House plants as well we love and they make the air much, much lighter for us."

Tarra: - "I do have some . . . not enough probably. What about near crystals?"

Fairies: - "Oh yes, we love crystals – very, very attracted to crystals. We recommend as often as possible you clean them and put them out under the full moon so their energy stays strong."

Tarra: - "And the little water feature I have, do you like those sort of things?"

Fairies: - "Yes, yes definitely, it's beautiful, particularly the water sprites are drawn in to there; much better than gutters."

Tarra: - "My gutters anyway . . . (Laughter)"

Fairies: - "We're going to leave you now; we want to encourage you to come out and play with us."

Tarra: - "Certainly will. Thank you very much."

Caz: "Ah, I have one final message. It's um . . . ah . . . OK."

JESUS

Jesus: - "I'm Jesus and I'm here to show you how much I love you."

Tarra: - "Thank you."

Jesus: - "I do not have any messages to impart to you today; I just want you to feel the love and affection I hold for you."

Tarra: - "I have a question for you."

Jesus: - "Yes."

Tarra: - "When I was with the Kinesiologist, she said my heart . . . heart chakra . . . or my heart was compressed. That's not the word she used but that's the meaning I got from her words, and she opened it out towards the front of me. Umm, why would that have been? I thought I was opening out more."

Jesus: - "You are, you are indeed but you still close yourself down. She is a beautiful spirit and she is to be trusted."

Tarra: - "Yes, I like being with her. She also gave me a brochure and marked one of the courses I could take which would help me to have people . . . mothers bring children to me and actually make them feel comfortable coming to me. Would that be of benefit for any work I need to do and is that where I am going."

Jesus: - "Yes, Tarra, I recommend indeed, that you do this and Mother Mary and Quan Yin would like to come and help you with this also."

Tarra: - "Oh, please! Thank you!"

Jesus: - "I must step aside because my energy is hurting Caz at this time, I have to go."

25 October, 2004

IMHOTEP

Caz: ". . . . . Ahh . . . . .OK. . . . ."

Imhotep: - "I challenge thee Tarra."

Tarra: - "Sorry?"

Imhotep: - "I challenge thee Tarra."

(Disconcerted laughter . . . . a little apprehensive about what the challenge would be,)

Imhotep: - "I challenge thee to reach into your deepest soul and bring forth that which has been hidden for many centuries."

Tarra: - "Who am I speaking to?"

Imhotep: - "Imhotep . . ."

Tarra: - "Do I know you from previous lives?"

Imhotep: - "You were one of my most prized Priestesses, Tarra."

Tarra: - "What was my name?"

Imhotep: - "Eva – that is Y-v-e."

Tarra: - "OK."

Imhotep: - "You challenged me then as I challenge you now. You were inspirational in my darkest moments. I couldst not believe that I could go on; that I had not the ability to bring forth the vision I saw in my mind. You were there challenging me; telling me that I had much work to do and that I should not sit on my behind (laughter) *but bring it forth."*

Tarra: - "And did that work?"

Imhotep: - "Oh, yes! I couldst not see that you have changed much either so now I challenge you."

Tarra: - "I seem to be able to help others awaken."

Imhotep: - "That is what you are meant to do. There are many times when there are words quivering on the tip of your tongue and in your pen . . . and I would challenge you to bring forth paper and pen at those times and just let the words flow. You will not know what should come but just trust as you taught me to trust those many eons ago."

Tarra: - "I will."

Imhotep: - "I show you a feather; the feather of inspiration; the feather of truth and wisdom and justice. You were a fair Priestess. Many times I called you forth as an adviser against the wishes of other advisers of my court."

Tarra: - "Did I cause trouble for you as well? It was a double-edged sword . . . ."

Imhotep: - "Oh no, as Pharaoh, my word is law however petty jealousies will always arise. You have faced this in this life; egos and jealousies but, undeterred, you know that the word is truth."

Tarra: - "Yes."

Imhotep: - "You must follow through with this, particularly putting pen to paper and word to mouth and trust that what comes forth is truly inspired."

Tarra: - "Aha. Has it been you that has been urging me to speak when I've been at seminars and things or was that someone else?"

Imhotep: - "I cannot deny that I had a part in this but there are more as well, particularly Metatron."

Tarra: - "OK, I haven't spoken to Metatron."

Imhotep: - "He is that which shows the light for you to step forward and to take steps one – two – three."

Tarra: - "Mmm, OK. I'm not sure what to speak to you about."

Imhotep: - "That's fine. I'm here only to remind you of the great abilities that you have and how henceforth you can use these abilities as you were intended."

Tarra: - "It's lovely to talk to you."

Imhotep: - "It's my wish to go now but know that I am around; remember yourself standing tall and regal as a queen by my side helping . . . helping me from the young age that I was when I first took the throne."

Tarra: - "Oh! You were very young?"

Imhotep: - "Yes, and I trusted you then as you must trust me now."

Tarra: - "I trust you. Thank you."

Imhotep: - "You can call on me at times; however, I am not as strong as the Ascended Masters in making contact. So be aware and just simply close your eyes and see yourself as the Priestess you were."

Tarra: - "Thank you."

Imhotep: - "Good bye Tarra."

Tarra: - "Thank you, bye."

Caz: "OK. It's time to break apart for a while. If you want to keep it going (the tape) for a little bit longer. I want to explain to you what Imhotep was like. Um, he really did have a struggle trying to find words because his language was fully Egyptian and I (inaudible) seem strong enough to be able to bring that forth, which is good. So, he seemed to have that, as you would have noticed, a mix between almost medieval language and normal and a lot of hesitancy but I could just feel how strong it was. I could really see you there by his side. I could also . . . I was being shown visions of you greeting many peasants and slaves who came to you for different requests. There were a lot of Priestesses who turned them away because they thought it was beneath them – but you had lots and lots of time for people of all different kinds and that's why Imhotep had lots of time for you as well. Plus, you were like an older sister to him . . . almost . . . and I think you'll find a lot more if you read about him. I keep getting like fourteen was sort of when he gained the throne but you know history??"

Tarra: - "Yes."

Caz: "Often with the Pharaohs you know that sort of thing (history was confusing) but yes, he was quite ancient so I hope we can find information. I have plenty of information around here about him but he had – I can see him being quite slim – sort of young of face even as he got older with short hair except when he'd wear all of the headdresses. . . but not shaved. And, apparently he thought that was a vanity of his . . . many shaved their heads . . . but he liked to keep his hair. He thought he'd lose it soon enough, anyway. (Fond laughter) *OK, that should be it."*

Tarra: - "OK."

20 December 2004

JESUS

Jesus: - "I am Thoth; I am Maitreya; I am Sananda; I am Jesus. I am many names and more besides. I am here to answer many questions and to pose some of my own."

Tarra: - "I'll be happy to answer any questions."

Jesus: - "I'll take yours first."

Tarra: - "The ones I was asking silently, did you hear them?"

Jesus: - "Yes, in the core of my being. You too have been many people and your greatest confusion lies in that you are not fully aware of who you are – the greatness of your being."

Tarra: - "I know it sounds strange but I would like to meet that person one day."

Jesus: - "It isn't strange at all. This will occur but not on this planet."

Tarra: - "Mmm, I understand that. I asked the question about our relationship in Atlantis and from the divining, the answer was yes. Is that so?"

Jesus: - "Yes."

Tarra: - "I'm so sorry."

Jesus: - "Just one of the many occurring events that make up the whole; these things are necessary. It doesn't make it any easier. You have to remember that no matter how great the soul or shining the heart, it's still human experiences."

Tarra: - "I understand that but you didn't fall."

Jesus: - "No, I too have been on a long journey. Not many people realize this. Too many place me on a pedestal and forget that I'm a reflection of the human experience; that I too feel insecurities, guilt, pain, anguish. I don't believe that we should try to be above this. Without these things there can be no love. True appreciation of love and light can only come through experiencing the dark."

Tarra: - "I probably have many questions and you will have heard them but I can't remember them all now."

Jesus: - "You'll remember what you need to remember when you need to remember it. Now I have a question for you. Deep within you there is a small . . . tiny child. Sometimes you find yourself looking at this child and feeling loss . . . feeling this child isn't enough; isn't wise enough; isn't protected enough; isn't strong enough. Sometimes you feel this child deserves punishment and this you mete out regularly punishing this child who is your soul. This is understandable; all humans do it but I want you to tell me now, do you love this child?"

Tarra: - "I don't know. There are things about her that I don't understand – motivations, even at a young age."

Jesus: - "This is so. On each journey in each life, this child so easily affected by all around and still searching and still vulnerable even when the adult stage is reached. That is ok. That is human nature to wonder, to not make the right decisions. In loving this child in loving yourself through all mistakes understanding that one is not perfect, not perfect in actions, not perfect in thoughts. Perfect only in the shining light of the soul which will only be rediscovered when you accept that you are worthy of love. There is nothing that child has done, that the adult you has done that can ever eradicate this light, that can ever stain this light in my eyes . . . in the eyes of the Lord . . . you are beautiful, you are perfect. I wish you to see this child as a perfect rose so wondrous and beautiful to behold that you wish to consume it because one touch of its velvety petals is never enough even though you know when touching the petals it may bruise it. That in cutting the flower it will die. All these things you fear when looking on to something so perfect, so untouched. And yet, in its natural state, the bloom still dies only to be reborn and through each stage beauty and love and light is present . . . from the seed to the blossom to the bloom to the rose head all is a natural, recurring cycle. There is beauty in all these things. Inside your friend and sister Sini was this rose and all who knew her saw this rose. Inside you is this rose but you have hidden it because you didn't believe in it for yourself. This perfect rose is also your womanhood, something that confuses you greatly on many levels. This confusion stems largely from the fact that you've had many lives as a male as well as a female. In this life you've chosen to be female so that you can be soft when required and strong when needed, always wise even when you feel vulnerable and insecure. Your feminine core will make sure you pull through all difficulties because the female finds it easier to tap into her intuition and into the spirit . . . into her soul. The poor males do this too but it is more difficult . . . they are so deeply grounded into the earth, into the planetary systems, into the grid . . . they find it difficult to disconnect and to ask questions and to rise above and see the greater picture as the female can do. That is why this life you are a woman. I want to know, do you love this child?"

Tarra: - "I have compassion for the child; I don't know about loving her."

Jesus: - "I feel the love that you have for this child, you are just not aware of it yet. You are in fact feeling that you are not worthy to love this child. This child is you so you are indeed worthy. As Thoth I sought to populate the lands with people with enthusiasm . . . seekers of knowledge; builders of dreams. My enthusiasm may have been misplaced to some degree but not truly because I saw into the hearts and souls of these people but they saw only their inner darkness and were afraid that they were not worthy. Because of this many mistakes were made in many different peoples and cultures . . . but little did they know that I was not seeking perfection in them but in them their humanness to acknowledge and deal with their lessons and mistakes . . . their self discovery. That is all earth is here for. To nurture us and to provide us with more lessons as we go on our journey of self discovery. As Melchizedek I could see more clearly the fears and I sought more to guide by shining example but I knew that I could not take on the world; that I could not teach everybody. So, I picked a select few and they went out and taught of the mysteries but by then there were so many . . . so many disconnected . . . could not see they were part of the greater light . . . . . . sought to others for wisdom. The same wisdom like the course as Melchizedek sought and I taught them that wisdom was in the things themselves not within me. But as time went on and the people felt more and more disconnected . . . they couldn't see the wisdom in themselves and they sought it in false prophets; in Priests who wished only to fill their coffers and have the adulation of the people. So, as Jesus I came to walk on their level to be the humble son of a carpenter to stretch my mind and learn as a pupil and not as a teacher. Then came the days when the pupil must become the teacher and I fought against it with my heart and soul. I never wanted people hanging off my every word . . . I wanted them to see what was inside themselves. They had the power to heal and to connect with the Lord God by any name."

Tarra: - "That's what we do now."

Jesus: - "That's correct, that is why it is time soon for the next coming. Maitreya . . . . Maitreya is your brother . . . your sister then teacher. He is the one who nudges you, who holds you, who pushes you with a friendly love. He's the one who says – "Who are you kidding; this is no reason not to go forward!" Maitreya is me but he is also not me. He is a larger group of energies rolled into one to focus the light more strongly – many different Ascended Masters rolled into one. Sanat Kumara is part of this focus. He sits as a planetary logos and guides from the Universe as do many other Ascended Masters because at last we have seen that in separating from God many different personalities and streams of thought were created. To bring people back to wholeness we need the different streams of consciousness to pull them back to the fold. You understand this?"

Tarra: - "I think I do. That is where the confusion comes from."

Jesus: - "That's right. It is like a radio station and all radio stations played only the same song. Many would switch it off because many do not resonate with that song no matter how beautiful how poignant the words . . . so, there are different frequencies different streams of consciousness for the different souls, one no better than the others, just different. The differences are to be celebrated not feared."

Tarra: - "So (too) the books that we read where everything seems to be contradictory."

Jesus: - "That is so. It is like the old pantheons of the Gods, many fears and confusions was caused as peoples migrated and brought their gods with them and encountered new Gods. It created a great deal of pain – often murders done in the names of Gods because of this confusion. Some enlightened peoples would see that the Gods were very similar to each other indeed. So some Gods were assimilated into different cultures and many of the stories of the different cultures were similar and many were different In accepting not the names but the deeds and the lessons as being more important we grow. We read between the lines the greater lessons and the greater truth instead of fearing what is right or wrong, who wrote this who wrote that, we gain the greater and we learn more because there is no fear. Because one of the greatest human faults, which some of us find endearing, is in always wanting to know what is right and who is right and not trusting their own selves to see what feels right and what resonates the most. It is like a child at school who will prefer to read than play games but play games because the others want them to. Because they'll be unpopular if they don't but deep down they are miserable because they would rather just read. It is often this type of psyche which causes some writings to be quite arrogant this desire to be the leader and to force others to be followers when there are no leaders and no followers in truth only all souls seeking wholeness and light. Look only inside yourself at the light, at the seeking child and follow what resonates with you."

Tarra: - "Hence the Reconnection . . . ?"

Jesus: - "It is easy even for these things to be corrupted in part. To stay pure to the truth of the Connection and what it means for you. You do these things because they feel right for you not for others."

Tarra: - "Yes . . . (point personal to another omitted). The Reconnection itself seems to be what is needed for everyone."

Jesus: - "Yes, the whole thing as it stands has integrity but this is on a person to person basis. It is like the Priests – some who have come to God for all the right reasons; some who lose those reasons over time because of what they see – the pain and anguish. Some who come for the right reasons but are corrupted by ego and power. Some come to God because they feel lost and pass on this pain to others and some who stay true to the light within speaking only with truth and integrity. But, this becomes rarer and rarer with the pressures put on these people because of the words of others and the deeds of others and so it is the same with healing modalities. There will always be those who are lost and find it difficult to tune in to what is within. Their fears cause the corruption. So, if the Reconnection feels for you what is right it is right."

Tarra: - "It feels right."

Jesus: - "For others around the world there are still more methods of healing – the sacred fire amongst others. There is none better than the other they simply resonate for different people."

Tarra: - (Points personal to others omitted.)

Jesus: - "All healings are personal to the individual and how they use it."

Tarra: - (Points personal to others omitted.)

Jesus: - "You have great difficulty in discerning what is your journey – and what is others. It is difficult to, shall we say, disconnect from others while trying to connect to all (amused). But, it is all streams of consciousness so it is ok. We are all one on individual paths so what is right for you is not always right for others and vice versa."

Tarra: - "I realize that."

Jesus: - "You do, you just need to remind yourself every now and again mainly because it brings up many fears for you that you are not helping enough people or that you are not worthy to help enough people. Number one is truly your self. Take care of your own needs and desires; your own lessons and let that self knowledge just flow out from you. Be that shining example and when you come to teach you will really be able to help people find within themselves what is right for them. I'm stepping back now."

Tarra: - "I thank you."

31 May, 2005

QUAN YIN

Caz: "OK, straight away I get a very special friend of yours who has been waiting to come through; she's been with you a lot. It's Quan Yin."

Tarra: - "Oh, is she a special friend of mine?"

Caz: - "Absolutely."

Tarra: - "Well, I have a question before she starts. (Laughter), I'm getting my bits in first today.

Caz: "She's . . . . . . She's laughing." (So is Caz)

Tarra: - "It's really nice to meet her; I've been so waiting for her to come through 'because I've had Mother Mary come through informally with C (another friend of mine). I'm going to the course on NSR with Peter in about two weeks time and are Quan Yin and Mother Mary . . . are they both coming to help me again?

Quan Yin: - "Absolutely, we wouldn't be anywhere else."

Tarra: - "Ah, lovely . . . thank you. Do you have anything for me?"

Quan Yin: - "I give you the symbol of the lotus. This symbol, hold in your mind at times when you need peace. I'm most impressed as is Mother Mary with the healing work that you have been doing and how you have opened your heart and your arms and your mind to those who are coming to you for readings. This is just the tip of the iceberg."

Tarra: - "Lovely, I'm sort of getting a little bit impatient but a little bit afraid at the same time and I know that's a terrible thing to say . . . . . . little bit apprehensive."

Quan Yin: - "Quite understandable, you feel as if this is something new; new territory that you may not be ready for however, this is simply you coming back. Coming back to what you have always known bringing up the ancient knowledge that you have always had. It is important that when you do your readings that you see deep orange and red flowing from you into the earth. This is not, as you've been afraid of in the past, full grounding, this is more an anchoring . . . anchoring of the ancient earth energies. Many of the people who will be coming to you have ancient knowledge themselves waiting to be awakened."

(A large portion omitted here personal to old friends and acquaintances where I needed some clarity about my role and in one instance where I felt I could have handled a situation better.)

Tarra: - "Yes. Oh well, I find it difficult when I know I've hurt someone."

Quan Yin: - "Yes. It's your heart. You have a very great heart and you really dislike confrontation without credible results. You don't ever want to upset people unless you can see that it is thought provoking in a positive way that will help and not hinder and this concerns you a great deal in all your relationships. That's why we love you."

Tarra: - "Mmm, well I'm pleased. I'm so pleased you're there even though you must have known what I've been writing over the past three days. I've had a little bit of a hard time."

Quan Yin: - "Yes, this is true and I'm showing you a beautiful feather quill. As you write imagine this feather quill in your hand helping you to release all that needs to be released onto the paper. Some of this is channeling and some of this is simply releasing of all the thoughts and darkness too that you have held."

Tarra: - Yes, yes.

Quan Yin: - "Very important . . ."

Tarra: - "Yes, while I have you here and while I remember. It may not be for you but I was typing one day on the old electric typewriter and out of the blue the typewriter started typing by itself. And, thinking I'd messed up my typing I started to pull the page out and stopped that (the typewriter). To my surprise the typing with the correct punctuation and all said, "Hello, I'd like . . . . ." Was that someone trying to talk to me?"

Quan Yin: - "That was me."

Tarra: - "Oh, (delighted laughter) lovely."

Quan Yin: - "Hello . . . (chuckling to herself)

Tarra: - "Hi!"

Quan Yin: - . . . I'd like to show you that we are with you here always and that you have a true divine connection to the light."

Tarra: - "Oh, thank you."

Quan Yin: - "This is what we wished to express and there was great laughter at your blocking of this."

Tarra: - "I didn't mean to."

Quan Yin: - "No, this is natural at that time that you would block yourself thus. Before I have come through with Mother Mary in the readings to let you know that we see you as our special project and this has not changed. You have a great and wondrous heart that has at times been clenched closed tightly for fear of more damage or harm. We are here to protect your heart with the help of the beautiful Archangel Michael who is all . . . our champion."

Tarra: - "Yes, thank you."

Quan Yin: - "This will allow you to see your heart as that lotus; to see it unfurling and radiant in pink and white and green."

Tarra: - "That's interesting . . . um . . . I had a reading with Cheryl again, as I've done over the past year and a half (when I go to the 'Mind, Body, Spirit' Festivals) and she spoke about this huge white light coming out of my heart from a large lotus with a small lotus in the middle."

Quan Yin: - "Yes, this is how we see your heart. Remember too, as the saying goes 'the lotus grows out of mud' and mud is so rich with all the building blocks of life. It is also the thing which transforms that which is dead and decaying into nutrients, rich for rebirth and for growth."

Tarra: - "Yes, ah ha . . . I have been, as you know, reading the Kryon channels and um . . . I know that time doesn't mean anything much but here it does and the time frame of the magnetic . . . um . . . shift and setting of the magnetic grid."

Quan Yin: - "Yes."

Tarra: - "I thought it was finished in 2000. From what we've been feeling last September (2004)and even this year (2005) is that the energy of the grid settling that we feel rather than that it's still being moved?"

Quan Yin: - "Yes. No, it has been moved. On the spiritual levels the energy shift has occurred. Now it is settling down to the physical levels."

Tarra: - "Right . . ."

Quan Yin: - "So you'll feel a great deal of change but also a, certain stodginess. A certain denseness that feels a little bit difficult to shake free."

Tarra: - "Yes."

Quan Yin: - "Some people are experiencing strange pains on their body and head. That doesn't last particularly long but causes concern."

Tarra: - "Yes, I had an unusual very thin, sharp pain line coming in under my heart and at odd times in my hands – quite sharp – and in other parts of the body around the stomach as well. Just sharp . . . . like little needles, like um . . . acupuncture needles."

Quan Yin: - "Yes, yes. This is the grid affecting your physical self."

Tarra: - "OK. So now, from what Kryon was saying, the crystalline grid or . . . is being re-activated, aligned or set in place, is that correct? Is that what is happening?"

Quan Yin: - "Yes, absolutely correct."

Tarra: - "So, in the past when Michael was near me, I would feel the tingling on the back of my neck but that's changed; I don't feel that any more."

Quan Yin: - "That is only a temporary thing. You'll feel that again."

Tarra: - "OK. (Small very personal part left out here because it would take a whole book to explain the comment.)"

Quan Yin: - "But you see he's here (chuckling again) . . . and he's been champing at the bit to speak to you as well, today. So I think its best that myself and Mother Mary, who is always with me at this time for you, to step aside. We just wish you to remember that we are always with you. Any difficulties you are having expressing love and accepting love . . . ah . . . and by love you know we mean the world."

Tarra: - 'Yes ok, thank you very much."

Quan Yin: - "Just call on us and see that lotus. OK. We allow Michael through now."

ARCHANGEL MICHAEL

Michael: - "Beloved Tarra how would you ever think that I could step aside; I've always been here for you?"

Tarra: - "Yes, did you see the drawing I had (done)?"

Michael: - "Yes, I was most impressed (teasing and sounding flippant).

Tarra: - "I see you as much more animated than that."

Michael: - "I wasn't sure that it depicted the amount of strength that I have."

Tarra: - (I laughed out loud at his pretense of vanity.) "It didn't. It definitely didn't but that is how the lady sees you."

Michael: - "Yes, I have to say that I have been accused by my fellow Archangels of being egotistical at times but I tell them that I'm just trying to take on some human traits so that you may better assimilate with me."

Tarra: - "Yes and that's good – strength is one of the things that I desperately need to feel from you; and your humour."

Michael: - "It is. When I look at you I see the Tara, I see the warrioress and I would like you to see yourself as thus too. When you feel passions rising in you, I'd like you to see yourself as a Zena the warrior princess."

Tarra: - "Yes. I often feel that way anyway. I do feel strong and needing to break out quite often."

Michael: - "Definitely, spear in hand you can conquer anything. Yours is no longer the sword, you've shed the sword; you are now more the spear carrier. The spear carrier is able to cover greater and faster distances than a knight with a heavy sword. You are really charging ahead at the moment."

Tarra: - "I'm trying to. I seem . . . I realize that when I have downs that its clearings and sometimes overload and I disappoint myself quite often . . . and then I don't really want to talk. Well I do, but I don't feel that I should talk to you."

Michael: - "You feel too often swamped with the amount of things and responsibilities that you have on yourself and you feel it will be a cop out for you to call in someone else to help you."

Tarra: - Yes.

Michael: - "But, any good warrior knows that he has to delegate."

Tarra: - "OK, you can all come and fix my house (peals of laughter)."

Michael: - (Laughing appreciatively) "You only have to call out and the right ones will come to help you with this but you have too many fears connected with this home and letting go."

Tarra: - "Well . . . yes, it's comfortable. I have it comfortable now."

Michael: - "Comfort isn't something that a warrior looks for."

Tarra: - "No! . . . . I must admit I'm very afraid of people." (In this case I was afraid of meeting new people when I move.)

Michael: - "Yes, that is understandable, you have been hurt a lot in the past but Tarra you know you have greater strength than that and what makes you afraid is simply . . . you don't like others to see you as either too strong that you don't need help or too weak that you can't look after yourself and you are having great difficulty finding the middle road with this."

Tarra: - "Yes, I am."

Michael: - "All you can do is to admit this not only to yourself but to those who really do love you. You need to spend more time expressing

the fears that you have, so they do not see you simply as a . . . . .
impenetrable fortress who they can never match up with. Because you
see, the ones who love you often see you as something that they cannot . . .
they cannot break through. That they are not quite good enough."

Tarra: - "I don't see that."

Michael: - "This is how they feel but you have not created this for them.
They have created this for themselves and it is part of their learning
curve as well. But, what they need from you now is to express the
fears that you have had and to fully open up; to fully open up to them.
There's nothing to fear from doing this."

Tarra: - "No. (Secretly doubtful)"

Michael: - "You can only move forward from doing this."

Tarra: - "OK, thank you. (Trying to end this painful subject but to no avail.)"

Michael: - "This is where the greatest strength lies in admitting your
weaknesses."

Tarra: - "It's not . . . it's not that I'm afraid to admit weaknesses. It's what I get as a result of admitting that. From one friend for example, I get a lot of hard line stuff that doesn't mesh with the way I feel and with another the moment she finds a weakness she grinds it into the ground. It's hard Michael . . . it is hard!"

Michael: - "Of course it is . . . Of course it is. But, by allowing them
to then be themselves and to react the way they wish to react, they
will eventually see that they are creating their own barriers because
in return they are not admitting to their own weaknesses . . . but they
will. This for you is all about setting an example and not pulling back
at the eleventh hour."

Tarra: - "(Doubtfully) I'll try."

Michael: - *"You have screamed many times before 'This is me!' and this is a good thing. It really is a good thing."*

Tarra: - "Yes."

Michael: - *"And I've been so proud of you."*

Tarra: - (Oh shucks, here I go again trying to hide my embarrassment and pleasure.) "Thank you. I'm still at a loss as to what . . . . How to help B and J? I'm not sure whether B is going to pull himself up and whether J is going to lose himself."

JESUS

Jesus: - *"Tarra, this is Jesus."*

Tarra: - "Mmm . . . (Jesus surprised me by stepping in here)."

Jesus: - *"Do you feel my love?"*

Tarra: - "Yes, always." (When Jesus' energy is so concentrated like this my heart area becomes very warm, not hot like the kundalini rising just very warm, as it is now as I type this.)

Jesus: - *"I want you to feel this love, let it fill you heart and simply focus this love toward J and B, and all of those you strive so hard to help. This unconditional love will have more benefit than straining your heart and your mind to find solutions for them."*

Tarra: - "OK, thank you."

Jesus: - *"They are their own souls."*

Tarra: - "I realize that, that is why I don't interfere as much as I would." (In fact I don't interfere at all and only help when asked but I used to worry about family members when they were sad. I don't worry so much any more.)

Jesus: - "You have done nothing wrong. You've only been yourself and loved as only you know how. Now is a time to step back a little and just focus the love towards them."

Tarra: - "OK. I'll do that."

Jesus: - "You have a great tear inside of you . . . that occurred when your darling Sini left because you felt so responsible on so many levels. And each time someone has left you, be it spiritually or physically, you have felt this tearing pain. You have felt battered and bruised. I want you to feel the healing that I and the angels are giving you now. (Long pause . . . .) Let us wash your feet; let us wipe your brow; and kiss your closed and eyelids and whisper in your heart and ears how very much you are loved. You are here to pass on this love to others. To whisper in their ears and their hearts and their souls. You are love; you are love. All around the earth there are many Lightworkers going through the same pains, most birthing pains that you have been through, trying to accept their divinity as well as their humanity and to pass this on to others . . . feeling a great pressure to do so as they are reawakened. The key to this all is simply love – love unconditional. See them all as I do as helpless tiny fetuses tied to the god-head with umbilical cords. Umbilical cords pulsing with light and love; none separate; none cast adrift. Tarra . . . . ?"

Tarra: - "Mmm . . ?"

Jesus: - "You are like a mid-wife watching over these millions and millions of little foetuses along with the other Lightworkers around the world. In every angry word; in every lost expression; in every depressed tear you see in yourself and others . . . you see the little foetuses still connected to the god-head but not yet fully aware of themselves or their surroundings or their abilities. Feeling the pulsing of the cord, the cord that is still attached to your navel; I'm so proud of you Tarra. You are my child and you have many children to look after."

Tarra: - "Yes I'm aware of that (I believe he is saying we are all his children)."

Jesus: - "But you don't need to worry about how you should do this . . . than to focus love and light. I feel you have two questions before I go."

Tarra: - "I'm not sure what they are so it must be another level. If you know what they are please answer them." (By this point I was really out of it with the healing energies Jesus and the Angels were directing toward us. There were tears of release rolling down my face that I was trying to stem so that I could stay focused but I just couldn't.)

Jesus: - "First – this discussion of foetuses has hurt a little because you felt cast adrift not only from the god-head but from your own mother. I understand this pain . . . and it is not enough to tell you that everything has had its purpose because you are human and 'as you are cut so do you bleed'. Just remember how proud we are of you and of your mother for having to do the things that she did."

Tarra: - "Yes, I'm grateful for that."

Jesus: - "The second question – is that you still have doubts whether you are truly following the path that you should follow and whether you are truly being of any assistance with the grids."

Tarra: - "Yes."

Jesus: - "My answer of course, as you know, is yes you are. Your mind, being analytical as it has always been throughout your lives, does have difficulty assimilating all this. You want to see the results."

Tarra: - "Yes."

Jesus: - "But remember, you can not see inside the seed. Even as the plant grows you still cannot see the beauty of the flower until it has occurred. I'm placing you inside a vortex at the moment . . . a vortex of energy as you are sealing yet another point on the grid right here and right now. It'll take but a second . . . . (Pause) . . . ."

QUAN YIN

Quan Yin: - "Tarra is it I Quan Yin again."

Tarra: - "Mmm (I'm a little bit out of it and still immersed in the energies of the grid)."

Quan Yin: - "Jesus is still with you . . . just . . . he has said what he came to say. I'm here simply to anchor you back again into that rich mud, rich and beautiful mud, cleansing and re-vitalizing mud; nothing dark and dank about it at all."

Tarra: - "No."

Quan Yin: - "You have just done great, great work in anchoring yet another point on the crystalline grid. This was a very physical one for you. In the past you have been involved with these mostly in your sleep. We wanted you to experience it more in the physical so that you could see and feel; so that your analytical mind can be a little more at ease. I'm going to step aside now so that Caz can come back."

Tarra: - "Thank you."

Quan Yin: - "We love you Tarra."

Tarra: - "I love you all – thank you very much."

(What an emotional roller coaster ride that was. It was a very long session and the first time that so many of what I call '**the team's**' energy was involved.)

20 June, 2005

SOCRATES

Caz: "................... OK .... *This is Socrates.*"

Tarra: - "Good."

Socrates: - "You knew when you mentioned my name that I would come!"

Tarra: - (Delighted) "No, but its lovely to hear from you again; I was concerned that I had offended you . . . ah . . . when I was trying to read about your discussions of the youth of your day."

Socrates: - "This is why I am here. I can't help myself when people are talking about teaching and being taught. The best students are those who query their masters who don't follow blindly the doctrines placed before them. Their open minds questing for more information, pushing against the barriers leads them on to be great masters themselves. It is the ones who close their minds to any but the way they have found themselves who will never become great teachers. For them, their ego gets in the way."

Tarra: - "Mmm yes, when I'm challenged I have a tendency to give in to emotions . . . . and hurt as well though when I'm trying to help. And, one of the things when Quan Yin was talking to me with Caz last time and she spoke about anchoring with the dark orange and red light into the earth. And, I thought that would be beneficial for one of my friends (who shared my interest in this subject) so I played that tape for her as well. She didn't seem to want to know that . . . . . . um . . . . . . and I was wondering if that was just for me."

Socrates: - "Yes, primarily everything that comes through Caz is for you however, your friend has some blocks up. Ah . . . she's just discovering for herself how many messages she can bring through so

receiving messages from others at the moment is getting her own ego riled up. She'll break through this barrier herself in time. She's seeking emotional balance before she can do this."

Tarra: - "That's wise as well . . . it . . . it baffled me rather than hurt. It hurt a little. I didn't realize it hurt a little until today but it quite baffled me because my friend, I felt, was really open minded."

Socrates: - "Yes, when I was a young teacher I was baffled often. (Laughingly) *I would find myself berating the fools, usually in my mind and to others, after class. How they wouldn't listen; how they thought only they knew best. But as time came on and I became a crotchety old man I grew accustomed to this and let them go their own way, find their own path and spoke only of what came to me from the Gods, guiding them only. It is like an old man in a field when asked directions he can only describe what he has seen in his own way. If the person chooses to listen to those directions and is able to place themselves in the eyes of the old man in the field they will find their way or they will find their path another way. It may take longer, perhaps even quicker but still the destination is the same."*

Tarra: - "Yes. I often think to myself and think back on the staff and the young people I used to have work for me when I was a manager and hope that one day they will understand what I've . . . what I had been saying to them. Umm, like a little . . . aha! sort of situation will occur when they'll say, doesn't matter who it was, "I heard that somewhere"."

Socrates: - "Of course, of course, how often do you say yourself "if only I knew that when I was younger"?"

Tarra: - "Mmm . . . yes."

Socrates: - "Always the way of human nature that we learn through experience and not generally through what we are taught. Some things are filed away in our brain and we remember them right when we need them but mostly it is with hindsight that we learn."

Tarra: - "But at least we learn."

Socrates: - "We do. The human condition is such that we are constantly learning and constantly evolving. It is those that are determined not to learn anything further who are stuck in a rut and will find it a more painful process to move on through this life into the next. I have learnt, well I should have learnt habit shouldn't I, over the years to disconnect from those that I am teaching."

Tarra: - "Mostly . . ."

Socrates: - "Mostly; every now and again I get excited when I come across a particularly enthusiastic pupil and like a new father I get frustrated when they don't follow my example but such is life."

Tarra: - "I can understand that, yes."

Socrates: - "I want you to know that this is part of the reason why we see you as a great teacher, the potential in you. Because in the most part you can look at your pupils, who you don't think of as pupils, these are your nieces and nephews and others who are following your example and are listening to your words while finding their own path. And . . . the older you are getting, like me, the more relaxed you are as to what people take from your words. Your greatest difficulty is with those who are your peers and less in your eyes your pupils."

Tarra: - "Mmm . . . yes." (Spirit always speaks of the potentials in us and I believe that in doing so they hope we take the broad hint in these statements and see ourselves as the potential fulfilled; the truth of our enlightened being.)

Socrates: - "And this too, I understand. In Greece, philosophers abound on every corner. Everyone thinks he has great insight . . . (huge comical sigh) . . . I found it so difficult. I would get my nose out of joint all the time. Then I said to myself Socrates, Socrates, you are only yourself. You have only yourself to blame if you have thousands of pupils who now think they are better than you."

Tarra: - "Yes, yes I guess that's so and that's ok even if they are better!"

Socrates: - *"That's exactly my point."*

Tarra: - "However, my ego gets hurt a little."

Socrates: - *"This just proves you're human. It is that saying, that came along much after my time but it is true 'If you not prick us do we not bleed'. We all have the frailties of our ego. It is our ego that gives us the thirst for knowledge to prove ourselves."*

Tarra: - "Yes, I've learnt over the . . . since I've spoken to you last, which is a long time, I've learnt over these last months that ego has a purpose and a place that is positive and its ok to work with that rather than continuing to try to stifle it."

Socrates: - *"That's so. Everywhere throughout time and all over the world men in particular have sat around comparing themselves – their philosophies, their strengths. Whereas generally, women keep all of these comparisons to themselves and let them eat away at their souls."*

Tarra: - "Yes, that's an interesting thing, that's the first time I've heard that from a man, that women bottle things up because normally women bring everything out on their sleeve but not that particular part."

Socrates: - *"No."*

Tarra: - "Is that correct?"

Socrates: - *"That's right, because . . . (sad sigh) . . . because women have always been shown . . . ah, spoken of as the weaker sex, they do not want to show this last vulnerability, they keep it well hidden."*

Tarra: - "I don't consider the women to be the weaker sex."

Socrates: - *"Exactly! . . . However . . . men talk too much."*

Tarra: - "Oh, ah, yes they do, actually they do talk a lot! (I got a little lost with his shift in focus.)"

Socrates: - "And they feel the need to compete against, not only each other, but the strengths of the women. Because, it is this quiet strength which has always supported them in all they've done and had them fearing that without the women who would they be?"

Tarra: - "Well, it would be nice to see the men . . . I've met a couple of men, only a couple, who actually feel the . . . um . . . usefulness of the power of women, only a couple." (Only a couple who admit it)

Socrates: - "More and more this is happening. It's taken . . . huh . . . more centuries than I can name for men to realize that what they saw in women as weakness, which is emotional vulnerability and emotional honesty, is actually strength . . . for men only discuss their strengths not their weaknesses."

Tarra: - "I've seen the peacock type posturing of . . . particularly in my husband, if another male showed interest in me and I liken it not just to the peacock but to the animal kingdom . . . and that instinct is still there . . . very strong. I don't know if I'm making sense here."

Socrates: - "Absolutely, in fact the image that comes to mind is not a pleasant one. It is of a canine marking its territory. A man when confronted with another man while their woman is around will do one of two things, in fact often both – 1) play up his own strengths and 2) put down his woman."

Tarra: - "Yes it's a very difficult, hurtful situation. (Tape ends – I turn the tape over while Socrates is taking his leave). (New tape) I'll say goodbye because I like to say goodbye."

Socrates: - "That's OK I'm watching (chuckling a little) I like to hear what everyone has to say because I'm a nosey old man."

Tarra: - "I like being nosey and I don't care who knows it."

ARCHANGEL MICHAEL

Caz: . . . . . "(After the interlude and with a deep breath and a small sigh Caz was again ready to channel.)"

Michael: - *"Tarra, it is Michael."*

Tarra: - "Hello."

Michael: - *"I knew you wanted to talk to me today."*

Tarra: - "I was . . . yes; I was asking . . . I was a little bit baffled about you saying not to pull back at the eleventh hour? I'm not sure I quite understood that."

Michael: - *"It is simply because your last protective measure has always been to shut down your heart when you feel threatened by others. And . . . when you are opening your heart to others endeavouring to help them, to show them a different way and they seemingly throw it in your face, your heart instantly protects itself and you back off. This is understandable Tarra however, there are times when as the warrioress, you need to forge forward uncaring of the pain you may yourself incur so that at last you can push down those barriers. But you will know when these times are correct."*

Tarra: - "OK, thank you for clarifying that for me."

Michael: - *"I'm so glad that you have taken the time to have a little holiday and I want to tell you that you will feel my presence over the next week, particularly by this waterfall that you will find. Whenever you see the light through the trees, dappling on the ground and yourself, I want you to think of myself and Gabrielle because together we are coming on holiday with you."*

Tarra: - "Thank you that will be lovely."

Michael: - "I want you to really absorb every moment of the next week and to lay down all your barriers for you will find much joy in other people this week and many things to explore in yourself as well as out in nature."

Tarra: - "Mmm, I was looking around at houses yesterday . . . but not sure why I was doing that."

Michael: - "The right place will come very soon and much sooner than you expect. You still have a lot of fear about this move which is completely understandable however, the reason I am here today and the reason that Gabrielle and I are with you over the next week is to remind you that your strength is great and we are always with you, you are not vulnerable."

Tarra: - "I don't . . . I don't know; yes I know the fears are there. I no longer feel physically vulnerable . . . um, my emotions are still a little raw, but . . . . Yes."

Michael: - "It is like . . . when your feet and hands go numb from cold or sitting on them, when the feeling comes back it is extremely painful. Living life is like this. We can help you numb yourself however true experience and true joy comes after you've experienced pain. You have experienced pain. There is no need for any more in your life as you keep telling us and reminding us. Now you have to accept it yourself by allowing your 'self' to be free from the past ties and yes, the magic word, the responsibilities and start afresh. And, even though this is going to be as scary for a child starting kindergarten, it is also an exciting time with many possibilities and many paths."

Tarra: - "Yes, I feel like I'll be so empty."

Michael: - "Oh no, not at all you will create a fairy garden; you will bring in the water nymphs; your dogs will love the place you find to call home. You will feel great joy each day you awake in your new home. There are so many blessings coming your way through taking this great leap into the unknown. But . . . you must leave the fears behind because fears do not protect you. Fears cause the pain from which you feel you must be protected. There is a woman with fair hair who you will meet over the next few months, in the area that you will call home. She laughs a lot; she has open arms . . . but issues, like everyone, that she is working through. You will feel comfortable around her; you will provide someone to bounce ideas off; someone to share courses and new moments with. She will introduce you to others but when you first meet her you will feel vulnerable."

Tarra: - "I always do when I meet new people."

Michael: - "Because you will see the shining light around her and you will compare yourself to her. And once again, you will think that you are not good enough but oh Tarra, you are. Her soul will recognize your soul and help draw you out further and further into the light . . . but it will not just be her helping you, as always, it goes both ways. So never think that you are less than anyone else because you provide great gifts to all you meet even when they don't want to accept those gifts, they are."

Tarra: - "Yes, that's mainly why I continue."

Michael: - "I want you in particular to rid yourself of all you still carry that is dark and begin only light filled things. Buy one item each week that will decorate your new home; something fresh, something that excites you when you see it."

Tarra: - "OK. Does this mean that I have to give away all of the things from my old home?" (As these words left my lips I realized how silly the question was – obviously that decision was mine.)

Michael: - "No, but you will find that many of them you are going to update or change or redecorate to fit more in with your new light filled life. And, like the people in our lives, you will be able to give great blessings for the things that you have achieved and accumulated over the years but you will know what it is time to get rid of and what you can keep as reminders. You need to trust yourself more; you are getting there."

Tarra: - "Yes, I still haven't broken down all of the barriers."

Michael: - "It saddens me when you are not cheeky Tarra."

Tarra: - (I let out a burst of surprised laughter.) "I don't want you to be sad. I didn't think you could feel sadness?"

Michael: - "I do when my beloved charges either put themselves down or put up barriers and hide their bushels from the light."

Tarra: - "Yes, I'm just not quite sure what I am going to do still. I mean it's still not completely clear; it's getting clearer and I'm not worried about that . . . just not quite sure."

Michael: - "This is the exciting part. It will all unravel showing you your new life in all its glory but you will definitely be hanging out your shingle in your new home and Reconnection Therapy is a large part of this."

Tarra: - "Yes. I need to do that; I need to help."

Michael: - "You know this because you feel comfortable with the therapy."

Tarra: - "I know that, I also know that I can broaden much more on that and I also know that discussion with people helps when they have problems."

Michael: - "Of course, and this is one of your greatest strengths. You need to list out not only the things you perceive as your weaknesses but the things that are your strengths you have to offer the new friends that you are going to meet."

Tarra: - "I'll do that. I'll certainly do that."

Michael: - "Right now, throw off the cloak that is the old Tarra; the old Tarra that has carried around so many burdens and has been worried that she herself is a burden. Throw off the shadow. The part of you that you think isn't good enough; smart enough; spiritual enough. The part of you that worries that you will never find yourself in a group of soul mates again because you will. The barriers are tumbling down faster than you can believe. You deserve all the good that is coming your way. I want to hear you laugh Tarra; I want to see you dance Tarra. I want to see you sing not only in your car but with your friends."

Tarra: - "That will come."

Michael: - "Oh yes, and sooner than you think. So, strap on your seat belt but remember always, even when you don't feel us, we are with you."

Tarra: - "I trust that; I know that. (Laughing) I get a little embarrassed sometimes that I'm being seen all the time."

Caz: "There's someone else here who would like to speak to you."

"Yes?"

URI

Uri: - "I am Uri."

Tarra: - "Uri . . . ?"

Uri: - "We have spent many lives together. I have been your father, your brother, your master and your lover."

Tarra: - Oh. Have you been . . . you aren't the one with the turban who was with me during the 'Mind, Body, Spirit' Festival?"

Uri: - "Yes this is me."

Tarra: - "Ah! I did want to meet you, yes. Well, I want to meet everyone but it's lovely to meet you. Do you have a message for me?"

Uri: - "I long to see you work with the crystals as we so often did and should you find a crystal, particularly the smoky quartz, I will guide you in using this for healing and the connection."

Tarra: - "I would love you to do that for me or with me. I seem . . . like many things I seem to have a barrier between myself and that ability."

Uri: - "This is because of Atlantis."

Tarra: - "Yes, and I forgive myself for that." (One of the interesting things to note about forgiving self and others is that, forgiveness clears the way and then I've found for me that learning to trust again is a much steeper hill to climb.)

Uri: - "Yes, it's taken us a long time to forgive ourselves but now, the crystals are singing again. They need our attention to help with the crystal grid work and Tarra we worked so well together. I hope you will accept me as a guide in this."

Tarra: - "I welcome you as a guide. It will require a lot of patience though."

Uri: - "No not at all, in fact you will find, sooner than you think, your connection to the crystals will grow stronger and it will come naturally to you. But if you come across any stumbling blocks, just call on my name and accept the information that you get unequivocally because I will pass it to you from heart to heart."

Tarra: - "Thank you."

Uri: - "Now, you've had some problems with your digestion."

Tarra: - "Very, very bad . . ."

Uri: - *"This is where the smoky quartz will come in. I believe tomorrow we have organized for you and Caz to be at the 'Crystal Castle'."*

Tarra: - "That's correct.

Uri: - *"You will find a smoky quartz there. When you find the one that sings to you hold it in both hands, sit on the earth in a position that is comfortable for you. Feel the power of the earth and of the heavens and connect them through your head and root chakra, ground them into the crystal. Feel the power burst from the crystal and fill you."*

Tarra: - "I just felt a little of it then."

Uri: - *"Yes, the crystal is waiting for you and you are already connecting to it. As you would say, you do not always need to physically have crystals with you however this crystal is a symbol of a new beginning for you, the stronger connection to the crystal grid work."*

Tarra: - "Yes, yes I felt that when Jesus put me in the vortex the other day. I felt it was like skimming a stone across water in my crown chakra."

Uri: - **"It is like there are many key holes over the earth and you are yet another key being slid into place. They are all turning slowly until the time, when in unison, it will all click fully into place and open the earth to the full shift."**

Tarra: - "Does . . . is 'Stonehenge' the final one or is that not the case?"

Uri: - *"Stonehenge has always been from beginning to end and it will play a major part but this will happen simultaneously in power areas all over the earth, including the Mayan temples, the Great Barrier Reef, the North Pole."*

Tarra: - "I have sent light from the North Pole. I don't know whether it worked."

Uri: - "Yes indeed it did. You need to trust yourself more Tarra as I trust you and as you trust me. Give yourself the credit you deserve; the credit that you have so easily handed over to others. I am with you as a guide. My heart goes out to you for the journey you have been through. I am present on earth at this time on the other side of the world. I am in the Middle East. There is much work, as you can imagine, to be done where I am."

Tarra: - "Yes."

Uri: - "And we have felt your energy and the energy of other light workers and this is making big changes."

Tarra: - "I read about the golden line through Africa, the golden light or the golden line – or the line of gold through Africa and it's almost like putting chakra stones on Africa itself. Do I need to remember those stones to do that; to send light through there?"

Uri: - "You don't need to remember these stones however, for you, holding those stones is more potent because you will feel their energy. Amber, smoky quartz, chrysoprase - which is pale green, golden pyrite, orange calcite and carnelians are all important for you at this time to ground the energies into the earth of the crystal grid work. You have been working very diligently, very powerfully on the crystal grid work but now it needs to be grounded into the earth."

Tarra: - "Right . . . and I do that through Africa?"

Uri: - "Yes, through Africa, straight up into the Mediterranean and up to the North Pole."

Tarra: - "Right . . . OK."

Uri: - "But Tarra I'm always here, so whenever you have any doubts about your ability working with the crystal grid work, simply ask and trust that you receive."

Tarra: - "OK. I'll do that . . . I will endeavour to do that. I'll replay this tape as you know I do these things many times to try to remember everything."

Uri: - *"I will never encroach on your personal space, I never have but I'm always here; always a partner."*

Tarra: - "And much appreciated; it's nice to know that you are."

Uri: - *"You still have great ability in sending through those souls who need to go to the light."*

Tarra: - "Yes I wondered about that yesterday when I was driving around, whether we would . . . with the magnetic grid settling whether I would be feeling their need in the same way I did in the past or not recognizing (it)? So I try to stay open; my intention is to stay open."

Uri: - *"Yes that is all you need to place is the intention that souls of the light will be aloud to pass through, to go home without encumbrance, leaving no residue behind. I'm stepping out of your space now, Tarra."*

Tarra: - "OK. Thank you Uri."

PALLAS ATHENA

Pallas Athena: - *"This is Pallas Athena."*

Tarra: - "Oh, hello . . ." (Delighted to hear from her)

Pallas Athena: - *"Oh Tarra you are so beautiful."*

Tarra: - "Thank you. (Spirit often talks about what I call our signature light in this way.)"

Pallas Athena: - *"You get stronger and stronger with each passing day."*

Tarra: - "I've been soooo waiting for you to come through again. I think I've missed you."

Pallas Athena: - "I have been . . . I have spoken to you but you do not trust in your own abilities, sometimes I feel like shaking you."

Tarra: - (Pallas Athena told me in an earlier, unrecorded session that she has been with me since I was eleven years old – the traumatic time of my childhood.) "That's ok, shake me. If I feel it then I'll know it's you."

Pallas Athena: - (Sounding frustrated and amused) *"I have brushed the top of your head many times and stroked your ears and tickled your nose."*

Tarra: - "Oh yes, well I know my nose is being tickled it gets itchy all the time."

Pallas Athena: - "Now you'll remember it is me trying to get your attention. You've been speaking to my old friend Socrates."

Tarra: - "I have. It's so nice to hear from him again."

Pallas Athena: - "I call him a blustering old fool and he calls me an old hag."

Tarra: - "Oh, but your beautiful, how can that possibly be?"

Pallas Athena: - "We do not always see ourselves as beautiful, do we Tarra?"

Tarra: - "No, we don't . . . absolutely."

Pallas Athena: - "I just wanted to let you know that I have been there when you've been searching for me and you really need to let yourself believe that what you are getting is true and correct."

Tarra: - "I think I'm starting to pick when I'm getting messages, now and again, but it's so vague for me in the way I receive that I'm not always certain."

Pallas Athena: - "You have spoken about affirmations and these are particularly powerful for you at this time. That you tell yourself," I am a true and accurate channel for the light", because you are. Repeat this often. You have great wisdom and you have a wonderful aura of peace. Now I know you may disagree with this because at times your aura has jumped about the place and you have thrown barriers up but these are crumbling down and you are settling into a wisdom stage as you bring back the crystal energies."

Tarra: - "Mmm, that would be so nice."

Pallas Athena: - "Water for you is very important too. You need to enjoy deep baths."

Tarra: - "Yes, I'm doing that but now and again I feel quite guilty that I'm using all that water when we're not getting the rain." (I was living in Brisbane at the time and we were in the middle of a very long drought. Again I have to remind myself that perceived lack makes it so.)

Pallas Athena: - "No, a weekly bath will rejuvenate your spirit and allow you to feel the weightlessness of the upper realms. Even washing your face and bathing your wrists will help you feel the blessings of the water, especially as you yourself are made so much of water."

Tarra: - "Yes."

Pallas Athena: - "I'm really pleased for you that you are getting some time away from it all and to just relax and take each moment as it comes."

Tarra: - "Yes, it was unexpected."

Pallas Athena: - "These moments are precious and few. We have to create our own adventures in this world. See each moment as a precious gift to be experienced, both the ups and downs, and you will find greater joy than you can imagine. Breath deep of the scents and smells around you at all times. Allow your ears to pick up the smallest sounds. Allow your heart to absorb the love and the light that flows constantly around you and through you. Allow your feet to feel the blessing of the earth and your head to feel the ultimate joy of the light of heaven streaming through the cosmos. You are a channel you are a breach and you deserve great joy, a new home that you can open to others, a new base where you can explore the world particularly the natural world; a new beginning.'

Tarra: - "I'm so looking forward to that. What's a breach?"

Pallas Athena: - "Ah, a bridge; the only breach (laughing) would be in your heart if you keep allowing fears of what is to come to get between you and the joyful possibilities ahead."

Tarra: - "Ok. It's a new . . . it's not a new concept but for me it's a new thing not to know where I'm going. Even in the past, even if it wasn't where I wanted to be going, at least I knew where I was going. It's a new concept to just let go."

Pallas Athena: - "It takes great courage and 99% of the world's population can't do that so we are asking a great deal from you. We know you can do it and you can teach this to others because there are so many who are coming to this space in their lives where they need a new beginning and a reminder of who they really are."

Tarra: - "I've been sending out God's healing light too . . . with the full intention of triggering awakening in any around the world who are able to accept that."

Pallas Athena: - "This is wonderful and this is exactly what you are meant to be doing. Even without the intention out there your presence on this earth at this time, like other Lightworkers, is allowing this to occur. But you, putting your seal on it; your intention for this to happen makes this more powerful. But sometimes you're going to awaken people before they are quite ready because they are in your presence so, be prepared. There will be people who come to you who are the last that you expect."

Tarra: - "So, should I not do this?"

Pallas Athena: - "No, you are doing what feels right for you at that time."

Tarra: - "Yes . . . yes."

Pallas Athena: - "In the long run no awakening happens before its time. It is simply that these people consciously believe they are not ready."

Tarra: - "Well don't we all feel that way?"

Pallas Athena: - "No some run . . . some run for it, rush head long into it however, this can be damaging."

Tarra: - "Yes."

Pallas Athena: - "You have found the right balance Tarra; you have so many strengths and abilities that you are just now accepting and it takes a great deal of courage to do so."

Tarra: - "I can accept when I don't have others around me, sort of making me doubt myself and yes I know that's my responsibility. I do take on that sort of thing from others sometimes. Sometimes it's a jealously thing and sometimes it's a control thing that comes through. And sometimes it's a fear thing that makes them feel that way about me. But, I'm learning to shake that off . . . those feelings and those influences off now."

Pallas Athena: - "Yes, it's time now to step up and away from this. You'll still see these people; be in their presence but step up and away and think not of what is going through their minds or their hearts and just focus on the Christ light and your role as Lightworker. The intention of allowing all people to reach their highest potential and to find their connection to the Christ light in their own time and their own way. You are doing this already but in particular you need to do this when in the presence of those people who you love the most and feel the most."

Tarra: - "Yes. My feeling is that I would prefer people to come to me (rather) than for me to go to them."

Pallas Athena: - "And this is what is happening. You'll find people hearing of you, people just being drawn to you. You have already seen this happening, Tarra."

Tarra: - "I haven't, I don't know that I recognize this except perhaps with . . ." (*Pallas Athena listed several examples of this – personal to others – so I can't include that here.*)

Pallas Athena: - "The list is growing Tarra, is it not?"

Tarra: - "It is." (*Comments from Pallas Athena personal to another excluded.*)

Pallas Athena: - "It is in triggering people that you do your greatest work. Your energy really awakens people without you having to do much work and isn't that the best kind?"

Tarra: - "It is but I would like to know . . . It is the best kind and I understand that my energy does that but sometimes I would just like to know that I 'touched someone'."

Pallas Athena: - "You will see it more and more. You simply need to pass more of your new cards and remember that the move you are making is going to trigger lots of opportunities but you have to be in the moment. Instead of looking to the future or the past you must be in the moment and fully experience with all your senses. This is the key."

Tarra: - "Oh, over the past few days I have so tried to bring . . . or . . . rather than get out of the past or out of the future in our linear sort of time frame to actually draw it all into the now, so that I can let go. And I've tried that and I've achieved it for possibly ten seconds."

Pallas Athena: - "You're achieving more than you know. It is like a toddler taking its first steps. There are many bumps to fear but there is great joy ahead when that little toddler is able to explore his world for himself and . . . this is where you are at now. You know there are many, many great opportunities and joys to be had but you are still fearful of the bumps along the way. You need to shift the focus and you are doing this; you really are. You still focus on what you aren't doing instead of on what you are doing."

Tarra: - "Mmm, I have little forward steps and a back-slide and forward steps and a back-slide."

Pallas Athena: - "Well, I'm behind you giving you a smack (laughing) on your backside to help you because that is the kind of person I am."

Tarra: - (I laughed gleefully at that.) "Yes."

Pallas Athena: - "Now Tarra, I'm going to go but you know that none of us really go."

Tarra: - "Yes and when my nose is itchy, I'll know it's you. Is that correct?"

Pallas Athena: - "Yes. Beloved I'm kissing you on both cheeks and on your forehead and now on your lips. We are soul mates."

Tarra: - "I suspected that."

Pallas Athena: - "Be well and be."

Tarra: - "Thank you."

Caz: "(With a huge sigh and a stretch.) Aaarrgghh, thanks for keeping me busy, guys!"

22 August, 2005

According to some sources Merlin is a title for a position held rather than a person. I don't know whether they all adopted the name of Merlin or not. I always thought there was only one legendary person. Whatever the truth of Merlin is, this transcript is of the one I knew in that life.

MERLIN

Caz: ". . . . . Ok . . . this is more than a past life . . . ok."

Merlin: - "Tarra, this is Merlin."

Tarra: - "Oh, thank goodness (laughing with excitement because I just can't wait to talk to a trusted friend – I don't wait but jump right in) Oh thank you, I can't remember who told me that Myrddin came through, it wasn't Merlin, is that correct?"

Merlin: - "I've only ever come through for you for Caz."

Tarra: - "Ok, thank you.' (That didn't really answer my question because my research shows that Myrddin or alternative spelling Merddin, and Merlin are one and the same. I felt it wasn't necessary to question further and the concern I had was dealt with later is the channel in any case.)"

Merlin: - "I'm here today because I want to remind you of a past life we shared. I want you to see this clearly and to absorb the energy because it is time to reawaken these particular powers. I wish you to see the deep Celtic forest, by deep I mean deeply magical and dark with small glades . . . . of light penetrating here and there whence we would do rituals. I knew you as a young girl when you had not yet had your long skirts and I knew you as an old woman. I would bring people to you who I had not time for . . . being a cantankerous old man."

Tarra: - (I laughed with delight at this.)

Merlin: - "Well may you laugh for you know me so well. You were abused by your father in that life; by this I mean purely physical and verbal abuse, the stripping away of your confidence in yourself. You were not a pretty child, having been kicked in the face by an ass, and you were made to feel unloved and unwanted by the males of the family. From your mother you drew strength but there was great sadness in her eyes because she knew you would not be accepted for love alone and she was concerned as to how you would live your life without a protector. For this reason she brought you to me."

Tarra: - "I have you to thank for my life then."

Merlin: - "Oh no Tarra, you have your own strength to thank. I taught you what I knew but you had greater strengths in healing than I. I have always been one for words, one for the airy fairy, for the connection with spirit, with the nature sprites, whereas your strengths are deep in the earth. You connected greatly with the light and the earth. From the earth you would find plants that not even I had found to learn their uses and you healed a great many from as young as nine years old."

Tarra: - "This is with herbal medicines?"

Merlin: - "That's correct, many herbs that in those days had not been discovered yet. You had to be taken from the villages deeper into the forest because you were called a witch because it seemed unnatural that one so young could have so many abilities. And yet these were natural abilities, abilities that many had which you had a thirst for because you needed something to sustain you, something to show you that you were worthy of life and love. This, other children did not have for they already felt loved and accepted and did not give any thought to their future. You felt the acceptance of the trees, the love of spirit and to these you were drawn away from your fellow beings."

Tarra: - "I still live like that I think."

Merlin: - "That is correct. Large parts of yourself from that life surface when you are emotionally raw. This past life is being shown to you to remind you not only of the deep connection you have with the earth and the light but the natural ability for healing that you have and for searching out that which is lost in another and helping them to find it again. But also, to show you these things to give you faith in your 'self' that you do not need to search for these things in yourself they are already a part of you. That all that you experienced in this life as in that life has brought you to be who you are today but you are aware of this. My reminder is only a gentle reminder."

Tarra: - "I'm aware of this; I have been wondering why I don't want to study the herbs?"

Merlin: - "It is not necessary to study that which you already know. In this life you need less of the green earthy plants and more of the 'trust' that simply by being, you provide healing."

Tarra: - "I've come to that conclusion that if I don't awaken myself that it will be enough." (At this stage of my development, I felt that being awakened was to remember and be able to draw on all of my abilities. Things are not quite as simple as that for us and yet *'they are simply that'.*)

Merlin: - "You are awakened. There is no need to search any longer. You have a thirst for knowledge and that is fine because I would never wish to close that down in anyone. I am Merlin. I'm always the seeker of knowledge; the imparter of knowledge but never more than anyone could handle at any one time. For you, you are seeking to fill yourself with knowledge you already have and you are afraid you won't reawaken."

Tarra: - "Yes, the stars as well and the planets and the light . . . (As always, I was deep in the energies of the channel and where did that come from but a forgotten memory of that time with Merlin)."

Merlin: - "You speak of my favourite subject. Many times we spent in the tower attached to my cottage perusing the heavens and discussing the ramifications of the movements of the stars. Remember that this is at a time when the majority of the people thought that the world was still flat. I did not wish to let them know otherwise at that time for my own purposes. It suited my self and other scholars to have others see us in awe."

Tarra: - "Yes."

Merlin: - "And, to follow their own paths on a daily basis of the sun rising and falling and the moon cycles which were much deeper than they could ever imagine. In some, it is healthy to have a little fear of the unknown and a little knowledge can be a fearful thing when people are not ready for it. You however were ready, are ready."

Tarra: - "I have some questions for you that I need to clear up."

Merlin: - "Yes Tarra."

Tarra: - "I know you, spirit, don't talk about others but I need to understand about Tasmania and the vortex that I created or . . . did I create that? (I was asked by spirit to create this and had no idea that I knew how to do it until I was instantly doing it in response to the request. It was beautiful, it was light and it was right! I had no doubt about that. It was not then and should never be something that I would choose to do of my own volition.)"

Merlin: - "You certainly did create the vortex."

Tarra: - "And is it damaging?"

Merlin: - "No not at all. You could not do anything damaging Tarra. It is not in your physical or spiritual nature. All that has happened has happened for a purpose. I was there in Tasmania as promised. I saw your vortex which you were afraid you had not created correctly if at all, instead it was a thing of wonder. Many souls departed through that space and 'many new energies' were able to come into Tasmania."

Tarra: - "I did see it when I was doing it . . . I did see it create . . . and I watched it fold in on itself with the gold light."

Merlin: - "The interesting thing about you Tarra is that you ... huh ... unlike so many, still doubt your amazing abilities. Even as you were doing this you were saying am I just imagining this."

Tarra: - "Yes."

Merlin: - "Which of course is not so ... the thing my dear, your thought is the power. Think that something is so and it will be; question it and it will unravel. This is an extremely hard lesson to learn, one that you knew well in that last life even though it took me a good six years to teach you. But in this modern world, where people say one thing and mean another, it is more difficult to keep focused on the power of the word."

Tarra: - "I quite often want to withdraw."

Merlin: - "This is understandable. Again, this harkens back to that life and other lives where you felt persecuted and alone ... and fearful of others opinions of you even when you have discounted that and thought – "Oh, I am powerful in my own right; I do not need to know what others think of me" – but deep down, very deep down you are always concerned about how you are perceived. This is not an egotistical thing; this is your inner child that little girl who was taken by her mother to the forest to the mighty and magnificent Merlin who learnt that it was alright to tweak on my beard."

Tarra: - (Trying to keep my glee hidden) "Ah, is that whose beard I've been pulling lately?" (I had several dreams over the past months where, as a small child, I was sitting on a man's lap and, fascinated by his beard, I was pulling it.)

Merlin: - "Now, now enough of that."

Tarra: - (I couldn't hold it in any longer and let out peals of laughter.)

Merlin: - "You're much large now and stronger than you were when you were six."

Tarra: - (I couldn't stop laughing to comment.)

Merlin: - "Tarra, I wish you to feel my love and my great respect and esteem for you. You have come such a long way throughout the centuries. (Coughing and clearing his throat) *you are making me quite emotional to see my little chick grow into a swan . . . for in this life you are surrounded by many more people who hold you in esteem than you were back then. And, as you walk among the every day people you dispense light without being aware of it and this is all well and good because this is how it should be. It is the every day people who you and others are here to reawaken gently and softly like passing out bait on a string beside a stream. There is no hook attached to that bait, just a little bait, nothing to harm. Just teasing them a little opening their eyes knowing that when they are ready they will come to you or to others . . . whoever they are suited for. Were there other questions Tarra?"*

Tarra: - "No, you've answered my questions. I'm so grateful that you came."

Merlin: - "I'm 'liking' those little wizard statues that I see everywhere. Caz has one."

Tarra: - (Laughing happily at his unabashed honesty; knowing what he was going to suggest. Knowing that he was offering this as we would give a photograph of ourselves to a family member or close friend because we know they love us.) "Yes, I've seen a couple . . . I almost bought one."

Merlin: - "I am much slimmer than most of those portray me as."

Tarra: - (I laughed appreciatively at his topical statement.)

Merlin: - "However, I wouldn't mind if you bought one."

Tarra: - "You wouldn't mind?"

Merlin: - "No."

Tarra: - "I'll try to find a slim one."

Merlin: - *"Farewell . . . however you know . . . I'm never far away and I may not appear often simply because I want you to remember that you have abilities in some cases greater than mine. Certainly less egotistical than mine and I want to remember that you do not need always to call on me because you have these strengths in yourself but I am still here."*

Tarra: - "I have understood that that's the reason why you haven't come through . . . because you wanted me to stand on my own feet."

Merlin: - *"Ok, I am parting because there are others wanting to come through."*

Tarra: - "Thank you."

For many years now I have had a dream where I was standing in a rubble filled courtyard surrounded by light mottled brown brick buildings. It was obviously devastation from a bomb that I was looking at. But, I thought it couldn't have been me because the eyes through which I was seeing the carnage were a soldier's eyes. He had a question in his eyes and heaviness in his heart that I feel to this day when I see this scene in my minds eye. The area was dusty and deserted and the wounded soldier stood silently gazing intently into the left hand corner of the courtyard.

Perhaps it was a memory and not a dream.

ELIZABETH

Caz: " . . . . . I'm getting a little girl . . . ." (Caz did not go into a trance state for this channel.)

Tarra: - "And who is this little girl?"

*Caz: "Her names Elizabeth . . . . She says **"call me Beth."** She has a lisp."*

Tarra: - "Ok Beth, do I know you?"

Caz: - "She was killed in the Second World War . . . by a bomb in London however, you were there for her."

Tarra: - "Before she died?"

Caz: - "I'm being shown you as a soldier . . . there's a shelter but you didn't quite make it there. You saw this young girl hovering . . . huddling rather . . . against a wall very afraid and not speaking. You pulled her underneath your great coat and ran towards the shelter but you didn't make it."

Tarra: - "Sorry . . . well . . . not sorry . . . (exactly)"

Caz: - "You held her close to you and she died and you were wounded. Elizabeth is here because she wants to thank you for protecting her and for making her last minutes feel safe."

Tarra: - "You are so welcome."

*Caz: "She says that you do this for a lot of people and that **"there are many souls wanting to come through now, to pass through yourself and Caz to the light."** She's opening this doorway for them."*

Tarra: - "They are welcome to go through."

Caz: - "Very good, that's . . . she was seeking permission, so that's good."

Tarra: - "They're coming through."

Caz: - "Ok, they're coming through. These are some of the victims of recent plane crashes overseas." (2005 plane crashes)

Tarra: - "I can feel their warmth." (Some souls hesitate with uncertainty and some are a little fearful but, by staying unafraid and trusting ourselves, trapped souls can pass through in this way because our energy field feels safe and comforting to them. Sometimes we can feel the imprint of their pain in our own bodies and from that know the cause of their death.)

Caz: - *"There are greater reasons for these crashes which will be made known. Surround them to just pass on up through your crown. This will be some from the London blasts." (2005)*

"Humour is the shortest distance between two people."

Victor Borge

ARCHANGEL MICHAEL

Michael: - *(Coming through quietly while we were still occupied with the passing over souls.)* **"Tarra, its Archangel Michael."**

Tarra: - "Mmm . . . . Hi!"

Michael: - **"Thank you for doing this, this day."**

Tarra: - "They are so welcome."

Michael: - **"These souls were scattered and frightened. We cannot draw them to the light we need workers such as yourself and Caz to help these ones come through."**

Tarra: - "I have a question about it if I may when it's time. (Missed some here – inaudible)"

Michael: - *(Still quietly)* **that's correct, you can do it now."**

Tarra: - "Ok, I don't understand how if it's known (by you) that this disaster is going to happen that the souls get trapped?"

Michael: - **"It is through their . . . own fear."**

Tarra: - "So, it's when it's an unexpected, fast accident or something?"

Michael: - **"Yes. Not all souls are trapped in this way. Some immediately have loved ones come to them and pass over with them but for others,**

when they are in fear, unable to see their loved ones they miss their opportunity."

Tarra: - "Right, well, I intend to stay open always for that to happen so please understand that they can pass through at any time."

Michael: - *"It is always necessary to remember that I will stand guardian for you throughout these times because just as the souls go through some hold back."*

Tarra: - "Yes. I think . . . just then."

Michael: - *"Yes, when you feel that – embrace them, point them in the direction of the light, I can then reach through for them. Sometimes you will definitely get impressions of who they are and their names. They may have things to tell you. You will feel if one is being particularly stubborn or fearful because for many the afterlife is an unknown quantity that terrifies them and they will not willingly move forward. Your compassion is called for at these times. I know that is not a problem for you Tarra."*

Tarra: - "No, it is not a problem. Well, it's not a problem . . . I have to remind myself that other people don't think of the afterlife as I do." (Compassion as spirit uses it is a little different to how many human beings have come to view its meaning. Michael is saying honour the soul's choices. If they are fearful or don't feel comfortable passing over at that time, then so be it. There is no pity attached to compassion. We are always honoured - never pitied.)

Michael: - *"That's right. There are so many . . . who think that they are either not deserving or they are worried that there is an end to this or that they are going to burn."*

Tarra: - "Such a bad thing that."

Michael: - *"It is, but you know that it is so far from the truth."*

Tarra: - "I know that but others I know believe in that."

Michael: - "The only burning that happens is in their . . . own fears. That is quickly resolved but at times creates that inner hell and they need to move through that and it takes our healers quite a while to penetrate that level of fear, but we do."

Tarra: - "There are still ones passing through . . . I can feel them."

Michael: - "Yes. Sometimes you may find troublesome spirits who are not keen at all to head for the light because they do not want to do any work on themselves or to help others and they choose to remain earthbound."

Tarra: - "What do I do in that case?"

Michael: - "Simply call me for protection . . . or tell them to what's the word – rack off!"

Tarra: - "Rack off?" (I couldn't help myself I let out a roar of laughter which of course lightened the energy making it easier for the souls to pass through. That is exactly what Michael intended I'm sure. Up to this point we had been conversing in subdued voices as we felt the energy of the souls passing through.)

Michael: - (Laughing) "They'll find their way eventually. You do not need to be bothered by them. They will simply drain your energy before you are even aware of it."

Tarra: - "Right, does this happen to me often?"

Michael: - "It has happened many times in the past. You will recall the two entities that attached themselves to you? These were such."

Tarra: - "Oh, ok!"

Michael: - "There is no evil intent, they simply like attention."

Tarra: - "Don't we all?"

Michael: - "Yes. What you are doing now is something all Lightworkers do consciously or unconsciously however, it is more powerful and potent when it is done consciously as you are now noticing how many are coming through."

Tarra: - "Yes, lots."

Michael: - "It is like a purging at times because, if it has been a while since spirits were cleared or a door was opened for them, there can be quite a few from local accidents . . . even cancer deaths where the patients were fighting it but a door is eventually always opened. This has always been our downfall, so to speak, that we as angels cannot help without being asked."

Tarra: - "Well, you can always chat . . . ah . . . and then we'll know. Sometimes it's a bit difficult to know what to do and who to ask for there are so many of you there. For example, over the last couple of weeks I've had such a terrible time with my indigestion and I'm not on tablets anymore. I haven't understood how to use the crystals for this or I haven't the patience. I'm not sure which. I'm getting to the point where I can't take the pain much longer."

Michael: - "This is understandable Tarra, as you said your impatience sometimes gets the better of you, which again is understandable because you work so hard for others that it is frustrating that you are unable to deal with your own health as you would like. Archangel Raphael is also with me. He's focusing light on this area for you.

Tarra: - "Thank you. I haven't spoken to him for a long time." (Archangel Raphael along with Michael and others usually assist with the souls passing through so it is not a surprise to me that he is also there.)

I thought writing this book would be difficult but it is nothing compared to the emotional journey, condensed into a few short months, which I have been on as I collate the material for it. Despite that I am grateful for the depths of the journey I have been able to experience which brought me to this point.

It has been my experience that when a healer such as Archangel Raphael comes through that no matter who the initial healing is for, we are all one and therefore we all get caught up in the energies of the healing. I willingly share all of my healing abilities and my healing experiences with anyone open to accepting them. So, for those who hold this guilt in relation to Jesus, get ready for the emotional roller coaster ride that Caz and I experienced in this channel and that I have again experienced just now while reviewing the tape before transcribing it. If you are willing you can finally release the guilt you hold (if any) which will lighten your load and the load that we have placed on Jesus through our feelings of guilt.

ARCHANGEL RAPHAEL

Raphael: - "Tarra, its Archangel Raphael."

Tarra: - "Hello. I'm sorry I haven't called you because I haven't . . . I'm sure I haven't been following your instructions enough."

Raphael: - "Oh Tarra, so often you don't call because you are afraid of bothering us. You know this is not the case. I rarely need to come to you because you have amazing healing abilities yourself but you are correct . . . at this time you need some assistance."

Tarra: - "I do."

Raphael: - "I am focusing the energies of red and rubies towards your center at this time. I want you to feel this warmth spreading through you. This connection you are having . . . this problem in this area is past life related."

Tarra: - "I thought it might be because it didn't seem to be related to what I'm eating (or doing) here."

Raphael: - "In fact it's related to the garden of Gethsemane. This is a huge, huge block Tarra and together we are going to release it. You have held great fear that buried in your memories you have let down Jesus . . . which is not so. When you think of the garden you feel great guilt and fear and this is balled up in your center. You allow this to also affect your healing of others. This allowing is not conscious but deeply buried. You carry a great deal of guilt not only for Jesus but for Sini, for your mother, and for many others because you feel that if you are a great healer how could you not help these people. However, and you know this yourself, for some the greatest healing of all is to be allowed to go."

Tarra: - "I understand that. I didn't, personally, try to heal those people but felt frustrated nonetheless to stand by and watch them die."

Raphael: - "Guilt over Jesus has been carried for a long time by, as you know, not just yourself but thousands; thousands who by holding this guilt have tried to hold onto Jesus. The love of God and Jesus' love for God was strong enough to push him through to the afterlife and be reborn even though so many held onto him. For an average person they would be earthbound forever with this amount of guilt."

Tarra: - "Yes."

Raphael: - "Your fear that you will never truly be able to help those you love or that they will feel let down by you consumes much of your emotion. I need you to focus on yourself as the beautiful shimmering soul that you are . . . one with eternity, one with God, one with Jesus, one with all. You are connected to all those you love. By flowing this love towards them without any concern as to how this will be used you provide the greatest healing of all. You have never let down God; you have never let down even one soul and will never in eternity. So, right now I am going to help you release that block; that fear that you are not enough; that you do not know what to do. We are going to draw it out right now and it is harder for you to let go of than you could ever have imagined because you have buried this so deep. It has become almost its own entity but we will give it love because this is human to feel these doubts and fears. Focus your every ounce of love towards this creature of fear that you have created quite naturally over many lives. It is as a child taking its first steps . . . wishing to break free but terrified to let go not knowing if it will fall; such is this fear and such is yourself. I'm taking this fear now and you are letting it go. I'm embracing it and absorbing it into my own core of light and like an exploding star it is no more creating only new life; new life inside yourself. As the potential of each new moment seeks deeply into your soul and you see that through only love, love for yourself as an amazing being of energy and light can you take the next step, can you find a way forward. Michael will ever stand at your left shoulder as a guardian so you need never falter or fear again and I'm taking that pain in your heart. The pain that feels as if it has been torn apart and I am . . . loving it . . . because that pain proves that you are human; that you have experienced much loss; that love is healing that wound. Now I am adjusting your third eye . . . which had shifted purely because of you inward terror that once reactivated things that you are not ready for will come forth. It is open now like the beam of a lighthouse. Many will feel drawn to you on many different levels both human and spirit. You have a great gift and that gift is being you."

Tarra: - "Thank you."

Michael: - "Farewell Tarra, I'm, always just a call away."

Tarra: - "Bless you."

DAD

Caz: - (Consciously conversing with Dad) "Tarra I have your father with me."

Tarra: - "Hello."

Caz: "He's um . . . a little bit sad and happy at the same time. He says he really feels so sorry for the ways he let you down."

Tarra: - "I know you do."

Caz: - "And that always he has loved you even when he didn't know how to deal with that or to show it or how to be the kind of Dad he thought people should be. That he sees everything that you've gone through and he wishes that he could physically be here to protect you but he knows you're a big girl; that you have many abilities and that the angels are with you. So, he kisses your eyes . . . and each temple and the top of your head. He's hugging you very close and asks that you remember that when you are feeling like a little girl to allow him to do so again."

Tarra: - "I'll do that."

Caz: - "I'm being shown the sun very strong and very warm. I'm being told for you to focus on that when you need re-energizing. Everything about the sun . . . the awesome power that it has over everything; it is the same power of God and the Universe. It is the biggest physical representation of it that we have . . . the largest proof . . . it is always there. I'm getting bye from all over the place."

Tarra: - "Bye."

17 Oct 2005

MOTHER MARY

Mother Mary: - "Hello, Tarra."

Tarra: - "How are you?"

Mother Mary: - "Fine, I'm very much in evidence in the earth at this time . . . helping to heal those who are deeply sorrowful through such loss of so many children around the world . . . through the earth quake in Pakistan; the bombings in Bali; the hurricanes through South America and lower America. Helping women to see their strengths and to move beyond their grief to realize the gift these children have brought us and them."

Tarra: - "Yes I wonder if consciousness, at this point, rises in certain people who . . . ah . . . haven't thought about these things really."

Mother Mary: - "Certainly, that is a large part of my effort here on earth at this time. Suffering, achieves nothing if people do not grow and learn from the experience."

Tarra: - "Exactly, I agree."

Mother Mary: - "Through the tears of the mother, as I've always been portrayed throughout the centuries through paintings, here the tears are the healing – the healing of not just the souls themselves but humanity's consciousness and the earth all together."

Tarra: - "Yes."

Mother Mary: - "Now, I wanted to say to you that we were listening when you were talking about 'allowing' to Caz and as Michael would say, "You are spot on!" It is very important that we allow at this time – that we as Ascended Masters allow you to grow at your own pace. That you as humans allow yourselves to grow at your own pace; allow yourselves to weep, to laugh, to scream, to sing because in each of these things you are working in the now; expressing the energy of the now."

Tarra: - "Yes."

Mother Mary: - "No one needs to hold onto the images of fear, of terror, of sorrow they need only to move forward thinking of what they can gain in doing so because holding onto those images of fear, of terror and sorrow will only bring more. But, you know this."

Tarra: - "Yes mmm . . . I do know that."

Mother Mary: - "I'm preaching to the converted here I know."

Tarra: - (Laughing) "I have a question, if I may?"

Mother Mary: - "That's fine."

Tarra: - (I had been reading some channels where Mother Mary along with Quan Yin, Kuthumi and others' energies are always said to be present and as I referred to these I asked the following question.) "Um, I have had some issues come up . . . can't remember them all right now . . . where I've said, "Oh, that can't be right". Is it the actual channelings that I have been reading – are they accurate as you see it or are there a couple of slip-ups where there's misinterpretation?"

Mother Mary: - "The channelings on the whole are correct however . . . as you aptly termed it, there are occasional misinterpretations as the tool who is being channeled through is only human."

Tarra: - "Exactly, oh . . . not ONLY human"

Mother Mary: - "(Sounding a mused) Also, this comes down to, as you know, what you are ready to absorb and take in at that time or what needs to be said to trigger in you more questioning, more seeking, more learning and sometimes these triggers are just that – triggers. Not necessarily truth but designed to have you wondering and searching for the truth yourself."

Tarra: - "Yes, I sort of . . . am beginning to understand a little bit, I think . . . about Spirit, for example (X) does exaggerate a bit sometimes; so does (XX) sometimes; so sometimes the stories that are based in fact as a human sees it are actually a little bit of a fairy tale – sometimes I understand, I think."

Mother Mary: - "You could say we are larger than life . . . (laughing) . . . believe in our own myths. These things are created along the way from peoples perceptions. They could grow larger and larger as more focus is put on them instead of the pure truth at the core. It is in searching for the light at the core that you'll find the real answer however, sometimes it is like looking for a needle in a haystack, we must admit."

Tarra: - "It is, yes, and obviously . . . I remember that I had asked Archangel Michael a question about walking out of this life body and soul and asked if that was possible and we didn't get an answer. (Some) talk about that with this new world but of course it's not likely if you don't understand the physics of it I guess . . . or the concept that you would be able to walk back body and soul to this life. Does that make sense, sorry?"

Mother Mary: - "Yes, it makes sense however, I have to admit (exaggerated sigh) like somebody who has no interest in cricket scores . . . ."

Tarra: - (I broke into peals of laughter. They know me so well. I dislike 'competitive sport' and in particular the running commentary.)

Mother Mary: - ". . . . . . I . . . its not usually my department and I prefer to work simply from heart to heart . . . and I have to say too, that Michael himself prefers to distance himself from those things. He likes to set the cat amongst the pigeons."

Tarra: - "I'm aware of that – it took me time."

Mother Mary: - "But – you'll find that more often Maitreya and Metatron themselves would be more likely to answer questions pertaining to those circumstances . . . ah, yes . . . I myself would not ask Michael those questions."

Tarra: - "You would not?"

Mother Mary: - "No, because . . . I couldn't trust that his answer would be that which I was really seeking (trying unsuccessfully to hide her amusement)."

Tarra: - (Definitely not trying to control my laughter) "Now, this isn't fair; I thought truth was actually truth but it isn't, is it? There's only one thing really isn't there?"

Mother Mary: - "Everything is . . . I would like to call it silver instead of grey, because we are as discussed, reflections of your own perceptions. We have so many human qualities because in my case I have lived lives and will continue to do so. But also . . . the other masters and the angels themselves are also reflections of the people who come and go throughout your life. So they reflect these characteristics and much as no individual in your life has the answers to everything, so too you will find us."

Tarra: - "Oh well, I like talking to you anyway."

Mother Mary: - "And we like talking to you. I want to say too that there is a growing affinity that you have with water animals. This is simply because there is a connection between you on a soul level with dolphins but in particular, a particular pod of dolphins which is now going up the coast."

Tarra: - "Right . . . ?"

Mother Mary: - "Now I myself, recently too, have grown an affinity with these animals which are so beautiful and so like us as humans in so many ways. Now the reason that you are growing this great affinity, why this connection is happening while they are going up the coast, is because they are working along the grid lines with the ocean which reflects emotion. And, you are working on this too but you don't need to consciously work on this any longer. You're just grounding your connection to do this."

Tarra: - "I understand. I often think about the dolphins and feel I want to go and see one – I've never actually seen one that I'm aware of . . . in this life." (I have seen a pod of dolphins since this channel. They were playing with their young out from Flat Rock camping ground just north of Ballina in New South Wales.)

Mother Mary: - "I highly recommend that you do so when you get the opportunity however you know too, that you can do this on an energetic level any time you want to. You will feel the sleek skin of the dolphin underneath your hands. You will hear the sounds of their cries whenever you wish but there is nothing, I understand, like the physical."

Tarra: - "No."

Mother Mary: - "So . . . if you have the opportunity and you live so close to the coast . . . with some places where you can go and visit them or a further holiday."

Tarra: - (Information personal to another omitted here. Mother Mary went on to speak about pets, in particular my dear departed dog Tinker and the fact that Saanu may soon follow him. Speaking further of my dogs.)

Mother Mary: - "Also, remember too that these are souls who've come in to help you for the length of time that they have decided; that their role in this life has been to be with you to experience this life with you and to be there for you. It is difficult for a dog, unless you are Benji, to go out and experience the world further than this."

Tarra: - "So, it wouldn't be a thing to give her to someone who has a big family or something – it wouldn't change – she's there for me."

Mother Mary: - "She's there for you at the moment but any decision you make will be made in concert with her. If you feel yourself suddenly drawn to doing that know that it's the right thing to do; that you are not just passing the buck, so to speak. You are not just getting rid of something tying you down. Don't ever feel that or worry about that because she will let you know if she wants to move on. Yes she does love families a great deal."

Tarra: - "Well I'll have to find one for her; I don't see why she has to die to let me move on."

Mother Mary: - "Remember this is her decision. If she chooses to do so it is because of what suits her – not what suits you the best but what suits her the best – and it won't be from sadness it will be because it is time."

Tarra: - "OK, thank you. I wish I wasn't right about it. Anyway, that's the human side of me talking."

Mother Mary: - *"She says she likes dolphins too."*

Tarra: - "Yes, she is so loving.

Caz: - "Mary's saying goodbye now."

Tarra: - "Thank you very much."

GREGORY

Caz: ". . . . . There's someone new . . . . . stepping in."

Gregory: - *"Hello Tarra, my name is Gregory."*

Tarra: - "Hello Gregory."

Gregory: - *"I've been asked to come to speak to you today in answer to some of your questions. I'll tell you now that I am from the 18th century. That I was a scientist and worked a great deal with cartography as well – maps; explorations of the world – inner and outer – as I used to call it."*

Tarra: - "Right, so . . . I'm sorry, I'm not sure which questions I was asking that need to be answered by you. Was there a particular question that prompted this . . . sorry?"

Gregory: - *"That's fine, I was asked by others to come to you so we'll sit for a while to see."*

Tarra: - "OK . . . ."

Caz: - ". . . . . . . OK . . . ."

Gregory: - "I'm here to assure you that your mind is a brilliant mind that has been through the ages. I'm here to show you that there is a greater world to be explored and that you will no longer be doing it from your home."

Tarra: - (When they say things like that I often think they have me mixed up with someone else.) "My physical home . . . so, you're talking about astral travel, out of body experiences, or are you talking about actually traveling physically?"

Gregory: - "I'm talking about traveling physically and astral traveling."

Tarra: - "Right, ok. So not having a home base – is that what you're saying?"

Gregory: - "You'll have a home base but you'll rarely be home."

Tarra: - "Yes well, I had an inkling that that would be happening. I'm not sure though whether it's to do with what will come as a result of something I do, like writing a book or doing healing, or whether I'm moving energy or whether I'm doing both for that matter."

Gregory: - "It is definitely both – these are things that I explored and discovered for myself when I was quite a young scientist and I am really a reflection of you which is why I have been called. When I was a young scientist I found myself writing of travels – places that I had not physically been. I wrote and wrote and wrote reams and reams of paper, of travels. Then, years later as I had grown older and put aside those writings as the fantasies of a young man stuck in an apprenticeship and unable to explore the world, I read in the papers of the travels of Matthew Flinders. Word for word they were my own. At first I was unaccountably angry and felt that my work had been plagiarized until I went to hear the great Matthew Flinders speak on his return from Australis and I realized that I had traveled with this man on an astral level. I was greatly confused; I wanted to approach him but I felt I would be taken as a lunatic. I realize that there are many things in this life that we cannot explain many things that we may never find the source of however what is, is. What I gained from my experiences of those writings was untold pleasure in discovering parts of the world that others would never get to see – that I myself physically would never get to see. My scientific mind really rebelled against this however I needed to know the whys and wherefores but there wasn't any and I felt that I was going insane."

Tarra: - "I have been at that point of feeling like that but I thankfully am past that now and understand that anything is possible."

Gregory: - "That is correct and this is what I discovered also. I realized that it was my mind that was limiting me and I found that my experiments became richer and stronger when I just followed my intuition as to what ingredients to mix together; to what process to use. In doing this I discovered some remarkable medicines. In doing this I was able to source information of herbal law that was not yet discovered but was later confirmed. By letting my mind flow outwards of my body and travel to those places where I needed solutions from, I asked only for the knowledge and trusted that it would come."

Tarra: - "Is that when we connected at that point?"

Gregory: - "No Tarra, we have not connected on a physical level."

Tarra: - "OK no, that's not what I meant. I didn't mean on a physical . . . I meant is that when our consciousness connected because in past lives I've worked with herbs . . . but, no?"

Gregory: - "I cannot see a connection however there is a reason why I have been called to you so this may be it. As I am now sitting in my laboratory aged forty-four . . . this is my perception . . . this is where I am. I'm sitting here looking at the fumes coming out of my test tubes and I am seeing a woman in a room far, far away from me and I'm knowing that this is in the place that I have seen in my travels with Matthew Flinders . . . but different. And I am being called to answer these questions I know not fully why or wherefore."

Tarra: - "OK . . . ok um . . . well I'll just fly with it then. Quite often when things happen totally out of context all I see are . . . I'm drawn massively to waterfalls and brooks going over rock and great forest areas; huge mountains and snow capped areas; birds and all of that sort of thing . . . all nature when . . . at the most inappropriate times . . . for example when I should be thinking about a mate or someone, like a partner. Perhaps that's somewhere where . . . . . . we may have traveled that way as well on the astral planes together."

Gregory: - "This sounds familiar to me. I have found myself often doing this too and (sheepishly laughing) put it down to being scatter-brained but I seem to work more effectively that way. I find it difficult to converse with my peers because now the factors and theories that they espouse make little sense to me. Instead I am always being shown the whole, the result and it is difficult to explain how I came to that place. Often our minds seem to give us fragments of the whole and this makes us pay more attention to our inner workings and our intuition and pulls us away from worrying too much . . . concerning ourselves too much with the outer. And, I feel for myself that I am shown those images to remind me that I can find any solutions; any information that I want within."

Tarra: - "As your own creator . . .?"

Gregory: - "That's what I believe they have been showing me. And when I say they, I'm not a man who is religious . . . I find it difficult. The churches doctrines don't fit in with where I feel I need to be so I've kept myself much to myself but I find these people coming to me seem to be garbed in light. Some would call them Angels but I feel uncomfortable calling them that because of my own beliefs. But there is no doubt that they seem to be of angelic being."

Tarra: - "Or they could be other aspects of your 'self'."

Gregory: - "I have considered that and I feel that there are aspects of that that are correct. Ah . . . it feels bigger, if you understand my meaning."

Tarra: - "The answer feels bigger or they feel like they've come from a bigger place?"

Gregory: - "Both, it is enormous . . . it is a feeling of huge connection with the Universe; much bigger than that which I see with my telescope."

Tarra: - "OK. I now understand why we're together . . . ok . . . I think I'm to give you some answers too."

Gregory: - "That would not surprise me because this has happened before."

Tarra: - "OK. It is bigger because you are a part of all of that. It is bigger because that's possibly an aspect but possibly . . . you may not like to call them Angels but they are creations as we created all of this. So it's just . . . it is you as well. Does that make sense?"

Gregory: - "Complete sense. These are little things that I have seen and felt that click together to make the whole but it still at times fills me with a sense of wonder that there is more than I physically see and touch. But, there is no doubt in me that there is . . . " *(tape ends)*

(Continued on flip side of tape – I lost a little bit here because Caz was still in trance state.)

Tarra: - "Yes, I had a point I wanted to make . . ."

Gregory: - "It is ok, I think we were drawn together because we have similar minds and souls but I think you are more focused than I am . . . I'm always getting into trouble for . . . my professor calls it 'off with the fairies'."

Tarra: - "Well that's true, probably. I was like that a couple of years ago. But, the reason why you can't see this totally but feel intuitively that you are a part of the whole . . . We deliberately did that when we created this experience on earth. We deliberately made sure we wouldn't remember that we were spirit, that we were God (a part of the whole). We did that so that we would have a focus on the human experience to learn about emotions and the physical aspects of everything. We deliberately did that. In my time now there's a . . . what we call a quantum leap or in this case a consciousness leap that we're heading toward where . . . that veil will be pulled down for many of the leading edge people and we will remember totally who we are. We know theoretically that we are all; that we are creators. Does that make sense?"

Gregory: - *"Yes it does and this is one of the theories that the local Theosophical Society has been speaking of. I have been to two of their meetings and I am very attracted to this way of thinking. However, I also feel it is not all for me and I'm taking what feels right in my center and what you have said feels right in my center."*

Tarra: - "Well, we can only ever go at our pace in understanding and knowing and I think that is why you've reached forward in time because you're thinking beyond the understandings."

Gregory: - *"Yes, I was only just thinking this morning that the answers that we are seeking now will be common place in the future and I think perhaps this is why I have been drawn to talk to you. But . . . I have to say it feels like you have come to me and not I to you, since I am still sitting here in my lab."*

Tarra: - (Laughing) "And the interesting thing is that I'm sitting in a friend's house and she's channeling this for me. So yes, we possibly haven't gone to anywhere . . . just that we've connected on the consciousness level."

Gregory: - *"Part of me finds this greatly amazing and yet another finds this common place. It feels right so I'm learning to trust and not seek so much. This would be a blasphemy to my professor – not to seek."*

Tarra: - (Laughing) "Yes, you won't be able to 'not seek' . . . I think it's in your nature to do that . . . but one concept that I've always found difficult to understand is 'everything is' or it's 'in the now' there's 'no time'; everything is 'now'; happening 'now'. On the other side of the veil that's the way it is. Here we have linear time where things go in a progression. Except for a very small percentage of the human race it (this concept) is still not accepted but, for that small percentage they understand how all of this is possible. We also know what, in part and in theory, the future is bringing because there are some brave souls who are pushing forward to another world. And, by that I don't mean this physical world . . . another world and I'm not even sure I understand whether it's . . . I think it's an etheric . . . sort of world."

Gregory: - *"Yes. I'm understanding more each day; I have been shown different . . . I think it's termed dimensions . . . I don't know what it's termed in your world?"*

Tarra: - "In our time it's dimensions but it's not actually a correct term – it's what we humans learn but it's a level of consciousness – dimensions are just levels of consciousness and some call it different levels of vibration as well, higher vibrations."

Gregory: - *"Right, I don't think I fully comprehend vibrations but consciousness I understand."*

Tarra: - "I'll explain a little bit about the vibrations. To come to earth in physical form when we created our physical bodies we had to slow down our vibration and as you slow down the vibration everything becomes heavier and heavier; it's not a light body as we know it . . . it's a physical body so basically as the vibration rises we become like Angels – basically. That's a very simple explanation of it – the higher the vibration the lighter." (Merlin says it's actually the reverse and then . . . well you can read it for yourself - 4 December, 2006 channel. I have no concerns about my discussion with Gregory – he is/was a scientist and will explore and then make up his own mind).

Gregory: - *"Yes, I believe I saw some experiments of the great Leonardo Da Vinci that were similar."*

Tarra: - "Possibly, he's famous for his insights."

Gregory: - *"He is one I have always aspired to be like . . . . I . . . um . . . I'm feeling quite drained. I don't know if it is this time travel or I have been up until four in the morning reading over the text that I have to prepare for my professor."*

Tarra: - "OK, well can I help?" (I found this channel to be one of the most interesting connections we've had to date. I had to reach out to Gregory and found it energetically draining. This was my first experience of how Caz must feel after each session.)

Gregory: - "I think it's just time for me to have a cup of tea."

Tarra: - "Good idea."

Gregory: - "Farewell Tarra. Thank you for these insights and I will spend some time trying to absorb them."

Tarra: - "Thank you very much for coming . . . or I don't know . . . or for having me."

Gregory: - "It's very strange."

Tarra: - "I hope I speak to you again sometime, Gregory."

Gregory: - "Thank you."

The whole time we were in channel with Gregory I could see him sitting at a desk in his lab. The desk was placed facing his work benches and a window on the other side of the room. The moonlight was shining through the window and expanding as it reached his desk illuminating the right side of his face and the room beyond. The window had security bars and the lab was one of those off the street basement rooms where the top of the window was level with the street.

This following channel provides great insights but also exposes warts and all, not only about and for me, but about and for the rest of the world too. I hope my many friends around the world are not offended by it and see the value of the information which helps me at least, to understand world events much better than I had in the past.

SOLARIS

Caz: - ". . . . . Tarra I'm getting the name Solaris, I don't know . . . . This one does not feel like it's coming in to overshadow me but Solaris is here."

Tarra: - "Ok, hello Solaris."

Caz: - "It feels like . . . neither a male nor female energy . . . very strong very high . . . very, very high."

Tarra: - "Can you speak to me Solaris?"

Solaris: - "Yes Tarra, I'm here."

Tarra: - "Hello."

Solaris: - "Hello Tarra, I work with Lord Ashtar."

Tarra: - "Oh, ok. Thank you yes, I have had questions."

Solaris: - "I also work with the pantheon of Gods and Goddesses. If there are any questions you'd like to ask I'll do my best to answer them."

Tarra: - "Thank you so I need to understand . . . I've been reading a channel and when asked, by one of the people in the group, if the Ashtar Command existed they (the entities) basically brushed it aside . . . well actually basically said none of that existed . . . but I think they may have meant past life as in before we came to earth. Is Lord Ashtar of that time when we broke away from what we call heaven?"

Solaris: - "Ashtar was recruited more recently than that and yet his energy was still present at that time but under another (name). Those who say that or brushed it aside as you put it simply do not have a connection with Ashtar."

Tarra: - "Right . . ."

Solaris: - "Remember that perception is all, some people have no connection with Jesus and yet he was."

Tarra: - "Really, Ok, with Lord Ashtar then, would he for example have contact with the Archangels?"

Solaris: - "Oh yes, definitely."

Tarra: - "And with Jesus . . . ?"

Solaris: - "Yes."

Tarra: - "Ok, so . . . but the people we were talking to like 'T' for example would not have had contact with Lord Ashtar is that what you're saying?"

Solaris: - "He simply does not work with him. Ashtar is like a General put forward by an Emperor. He has his place and he has his mission to perform."

Tarra: - "Ok so, when you say recruited, by whom?"

Solaris: - "By God . . ."

Tarra: - "God . . . but . . . I am/we are God." (Hard to explain what is meant by this. My belief is that here is no separation except that created by perception.)

Solaris: - "That's correct."

Tarra: - "Ok so, by the human race?"

Solaris: - "By . . . the Archangels and Ascended Masters . . . for the human race."

Tarra: - "For the human race . . . because Lord Ashtar is supposed to be . . . a group . . . with the Ascended Masters from what I understand . . . he's supposed to be with that group?"

Solaris: - "Yes."

Tarra: - "Ok . . . . Ok . . . . So do I have a lineage connection to Lord Ashtar?"

Solaris: - "Yes. Yes in fact, if DNA tests were done this would be seen."

Tarra: - "Ok, I thought so." (Too engrossed to ask whether the test would prove personal or planetary lineage; I am of the Pleiades system).

Solaris: - "In fact Iridology would also show similarities."

Tarra: - "Sorry, what's Iridology?" (I know this but keep forgetting.)

Solaris: - "Eyes . . . study of the eyes."

Tarra: - "Ok, so I actually still work with him now, with Lord Ashtar and the Ashtar Command now?"

Solaris: - "Yes."

Tarra: - "And . . . I'm not conscious of that . . . (at the times when I'm working with him)

Solaris: - "No."

Tarra: - . . . and I don't seem to remember any of it although I saw a shadow (shadowy figure of him standing next to me quite often) . . . shadows of him."

Solaris: - "This is true for most who work with Ashtar and the Ashtar Command."

Tarra: - "That's ok, I've sort of not tried to remember but in not trying to remember anything or bring anything into the now I've lost all of my dreams . . . nearly all of my dreams and am having difficulty bringing them back."

Solaris: - "You'll receive what you need to receive through dreams and what you feel capable of absorbing at that time. As frustrating as humans find this that is how things are at the moment for you. There are many times in your dream state where you have performed missions with Ashtar speaking to . . . . what you would term diplomatic missions from other dimensions as well as continents."

Tarra: - "Yes . . . here on earth?'

Solaris: - "Earth and beyond . . ."

Tarra: - "Yes but the continents here on earth, yes. I actually understand that that was . . . someone told me about that in a talk with Ashtar . . . can't remember who it was (Cheryl – a reader at the Mind Body Spirit Festival) . . . so I understood that that would possibly be in the future but it's actually happening on the different levels of consciousness with me."

Solaris: - "That's correct."

Tarra: - "And for you, are you like a go between so that we can communicate with Lord Ashtar is that right – you work with him?"

Solaris: - "I work among the planetary logos. I am a reflection of the sun . . . the great energy of the sun. I am like a bridge between the physical of the sun and the spiritual."

Tarra: - "Right, I think I understand, a bit like a conduit?"

Solaris: - "Yes, I've been known by many names in the pantheon of the Gods. All of the sun Gods are reflections of me."

Tarra: - "Ra and all of that . . . you mean?"

Solaris: - "Yes or if you prefer I am reflections of them."

Tarra: - "So, in order to send a message to Lord Ashtar from me as I am now, this aspect of me, I would talk to you is that correct?"

Solaris: - "No, I am simply another who works with Lord Ashtar and I was sent to help explain it. I'm having difficulty coming to your level I will admit."

Tarra: - "Yes, well I should try to come up to yours, shouldn't I?" (I quite often get caught in the swirling energies with Caz. The messages come through loud and clear on the tape later. To my senses however, at the time of the channel they often feel obscure. That is why in the opening part of a channel the dialogue seems hesitant and I can sometimes seem to be obtuse until I get used to the energies. Of course sometimes I am obtuse.)

Solaris: - "Perhaps a way to explain why I have come to you instead of Ashtar is that . . . like on a human level if you had heard of somebody who was healing who was quite well known but you didn't know what to make of this person . . . you would either go to see them yourself or you would ask somebody else who had experience with them. This is the closest example I can give. Ashtar is in contact with you often in a dream state but in a physical state he has many protections around that we have insisted upon simply because his role is so enormous. He is like the head of the United Nations."

Tarra: - "Right, so he facilitates sort of diplomatic things on the other levels and . . ."

We said together ***"throughout the Universe."*** (A portion personal to others left out here.) Solaris went on to talk of some entities in the Universe.

Tarra: - "These other entities or whatever they are, they are God as well?"

Solaris: - "Yes, but they are not aware that they are of God."

Tarra: - "Ah!"

Solaris: - "In fact they rebel against this."

Tarra: - "Ok, so are we talking about souls or are we talking about humans or are we talking about both?"

Solaris: - *"They are not human but they are souled."*

Tarra: - "Yes, oh, you might be able to answer another question there. This might be . . . talking about souled people like . . . I was explaining to Caz that I read a channel in which the entity talks about Hitler and Abraham Lincoln as unsouled beings. Do you know about that?"

Solaris: - *"Yes although the explanation was not quite as it should be."*

Tarra: - "Ok, may I learn more about that?"

Solaris: - *"Yes. Hitler, Abraham, and a good many more souls were directly following a plan, an order put in place for them by a larger over-group. There were often decisions made in which the soul stepped out however the soul was always conscious of what those decisions were that were being made at that time. The soul worked in concert with the greater over-soul group."*

Tarra: - "Ok, is that similar to Jesus as . . . I know was his own soul but . . . with the over-shadowing of Christ, is that a similar thing?"

Solaris: - *"Yes, it is a similar thing however this is a group over-shadowing."*

Tarra: - "Ok, so why . . . why would a group . . . were they of God for Hitler?"

Solaris: - *"Yes, of God."*

Tarra: - "Why would a group do that?"

Solaris: - *"By this do you mean the atrocities?"*

Tarra: - "Yes. Is that purely for what the Jewish . . . um . . . family decided to do to clear energies; was that purely for that reason or was it for a world reason?"

Solaris: - "It was purely for a world reason. All other consequences which filtered down to individuals and generations were . . . simply a by-product although expected and important of the greater world consequence. You will see or recall that at the time of Hitler the world was largely separate?"

Tarra: - "Yes."

Solaris: - "There was little contact between countries. Europe had more contact with other countries than most insomuch that they also held onto many past grudges and anger between races. The greater world had no knowledge of this on the whole. The depth of the emotions that had been buried and poisoning the earth and the spiritual consciousness needed to be exposed. Hitler exposed this."

Tarra: - "Yes ok . . . ok" (Much as I was resisting this I was beginning to understand)

Solaris: - "For many, it made them look strongly at their own motivations and their own beliefs systems in a way that had not been done since Christ."

Tarra: - "The Jews, you mean, not just Europe . . . or all . . . . . of the world . . .?"

Solaris: - "All of the world"

Tarra: - "But it also made the consciousness . . . . of what was going on with the rest of the world."

Solaris: - "Yes this filtered . . . you have to see this filtered down to countries who were not previously really affected by the second world war. You will see that Nazis moved to South America, South Africa spreading their, as some would call, noxious belief systems."

Tarra: - "And here in Australia; there are some here."

Solaris: - "That is correct. You will see that they fanned out all over the world and this was like exposing sores because in all cultures there is racism – all cultures."

Tarra: - "Yes, I find that even in myself."

Solaris: - "Yes."

Tarra: - "Odd that."

Solaris: - "It is like . . . ah . . . a boil is a canker drawing out the poisons from the body. So was Hitler and his minions and there is still evidence of similar thinking today but none on the global scale exposed by Hitler."

Tarra: - "No. I was thinking of some of the countries that are at war at the moment, not so much Israel although that is a huge thing that needs to be cleared obviously and that's happening but in the other (areas) near . . . not K (my geography is not the best so Solaris came to my rescue) but around those areas."

Solaris: - "Places like the Congo and Korea many, many places still in Russia and in America even in Australia, so many. There are still people fighting against their nature and their nature is to recognize all the other souls in the world but their nature also is to push themselves forward. But, so many do not realize that they can push themselves forward without taking from others."

Tarra: - "Yes, I have a huge . . . not as huge as it could be because I wonder about it but . . . I have this huge resentment towards America for forcing their ways around the world. I understand that they're forward thinking but their arrogance sometimes causes problems with others trying to find their feet. It's a little bit like when you're learning to do something and you're doing really, really well and then someone comes along who does it so much better (through past experience) without even thinking about it and belittles what you've achieved. And, I feel the world responds to

America particularly in the third world countries with resentment and their third world thinking ways of solving problems with violence."

Solaris: - "Can I explain on a level that would be fitting at this time?"

Tarra: - "Ok."

Solaris: - "America is a young country although not as young as Australia as far as civilization is concerned. We wish you to see that the Americans are the Indigo's of the world."

Tarra: - "Ok."

Solaris: - "The Australians are the crystals of the world."

Tarra: - "Oh, I understand, Ok."

Solaris: - "For this reason globally . . . I will show you further. America came from England which was an Empire . . . Empirical men thirsty to prove their worth were those who settled much of America. They still hold this thought but not the thoughts of the past where one Empire succeeds another. In America's heart and soul it is the Empire; it is the ruler of the world because they are still young in the terms of the rest of the world, in particular Europe."

Tarra: - "Yes."

Solaris: - "If you look throughout history you will see that the time span of America is similar to the time span of the Saxons ruling England or the Normans ruling England. Only, they have no others to try and take their borders so their wars are mainly within but they will not acknowledge them. Australia as the Crystals wishes to help the Indigos right the wrongs of the world however they are aware that the Indigo is brash and unthinking and rushes in without paying attention to emotional needs of those they are thinking they are helping."

Tarra: - "Yes, I understand that so well. That explains it much better so actually their purpose was to shake up the world."

Solaris: - "Oh definitely, America has a huge, huge place in shaking up the world and exposing so many of the sores in the world . . . examples of course Vietnam, Korea, and also many of the happenings in South America. Down the line we now come to a time where, those who have admired America's ability to shake up the dictators of the world, they are now seeing the underbelly whereby . . . it is human . . .and full of human souls endeavouring to do their own best for themselves and their own individual families before the greater world."

Tarra: - "Yes."

Solaris: - "This happens in all countries but the spotlight is on America at this time. For this reason were the great hurricanes in the south of America. For this reason the hurricanes and the flooding and the tears of the world."

Tarra: - "Because, from what I see, they needed to focus in a different way with their emotions – bring their emotions into play or not so much their emotions but their compassion for humanity."

Solaris: - "Yes, they're . . . do not write the Indigos off. They do have compassion for humanity but their anger is often greater and overshadows it."

Tarra: - "So this is balancing it, yes?"

Solaris: - "This is balancing it and . . . (tape ends)

I can't remember the remainder 'word for word' so won't include it here.

I have learnt when in session with spirit that one must be prepared for anything. I thought I was until faced with the following one which embarrassed me whilst at the same time delighted both Caz and I. I wonder if the light we emit that is visible to spirit glows and extra shade of pink when we are embarrassed? Venus embarrassed me a little but Mars went all out!

5 December, 2005

VENUS

Caz: - "................. OK, we've got Venus coming through. I feel her coming . . . she's like coming . . . (laughing) . . . from Venus."

(Every other time Caz channeled Venus she was already with us in the room so this was a little outside our experience of her and I should have been warned by that.)

Venus: - "Tarra, how are you today?"

Tarra: - "Very well thank you, how are you?"

Venus: - "Beautiful."

Tarra: - "That's lovely; oh . . . I'm sure you are. How is the work going with balancing the male/female energies?"

Venus: - "I've had to shove Mars aside; he's had his time in the limelight."

Tarra: - (Laughing with her) "I wondered about that."

Venus: - "I'm very happy at the moment because more and more of the males of this earth are being able to balance their feminine energy. For too long they have pushed it aside. Mars has been working with me to bring forward that clearer balance so that males can know that yes, we require their strength but we also require their peace and their love."

Tarra: - "Mmm . . ."

Venus: - "I can see the beauty within you. You know this beauty; you have often felt confident of it, this warrior princess within you."

Tarra: - "Yes."

Venus: - "Your sexuality is strong and burns deep at your core but it is like the flames have got lower and lower. There are fears in there but they are fears that you have confronted, fears that you recognize and that you can move beyond. There is no hurry, no rush. These flames will be re-ignited when you wish."

Tarra: - "I think so. I think a lot of the fears I have around that sort of relationship and allowing that energy to come forward again are . . . um . . . I'm possibly able to handle better, one because I'm older and the human males won't be . . . like bees around the honey pot again . . ."

"(Laughter from Venus)"

Tarra: - "It'll be easier . . . . . ." (Laughing with her – she's very happy today)

Venus: - (Amused interjection from Venus) "So you say."

Tarra: - "It'll be easier just to attract one who is attracted to me rather than my sexuality."

Venus: - "I think you will be surprised to see how many bees will be attracted to your honey pot."

Tarra: - "Oh really, oh no . . . (this is not at all what I meant now I am embarrassed).

Venus: - "However . . . you are well tuned, and yes indeed, it will be one in particular who you will be most closely drawn to and you will not notice the others at all; they will fall by the wayside."

Tarra: - "Very good; I have always . . . . within my being . . . .
Sexuality and love have sort of been hand in hand . . . if I tried other ways
that hasn't worked (was disappointing)."

Venus: - *"That's right . . . hand in hand as you say, Mars and Venus
together . . . because of course sexuality is also a large part of Mars'
energy. Truly either of our energies alone does not create the fireworks
necessary to the true meaning of two souls."*

Tarra: - "No, I agree . . . I agree."

Venus: - *"I think you have been a powerful teacher, throughout your
life, of this. You have a commanding presence of strength of the male
side and of intuition from the female. Very few people have been able
to pull the wool over your eyes or been able to intimidate you because
you hold a nearly perfect balance of the male and female."*

Tarra: - "OK. Sometimes I feel it's almost perfect . . . sometimes . . . balance
I mean."

Venus: - *(Amused) "I say nearly perfect because this of course is what
you perceive. All things . . . they're balanced or the life would not be
able to continue but . . . it is perceptions that influence this on the
physical level."*

Tarra: - "Yes. Mmm, I understand that. Caz and I were also talking . . . I
don't know whether this is for you but we were talking about the balance
between being spirit and human. Like . . . having that balance again it
seems to be the same thing of trying to . . . both are strong in different
ways and can tip the balance. And, quite often mine is towards my spiritual
side rather than integrating my human aspects."

Venus: - *"This is true . . . it is, as I would say, a beautiful thing to
be of spirit and to feel the love of spiritual love. You can feel this on
many levels it is a joyful, beautiful, perfect thing. On the other hand,
physical love that has your heart beating faster, your skin getting
hotter, your face becoming flushed is also a beautiful thing. So in all*

things in life, both the physical and the spiritual draw us and we often fear more of one or the other. So while . . . you experience the physical you are missing the spiritual and believing that perhaps you are being too base by feeling the physical and not the spiritual. And, when you start to touch, as in an orgasm, on the spiritual level you pull yourself back from the edge because of fear of what it would be like to move fully into the spiritual . . . to lose yourself completely. Again, in the spiritual level . . . you are fearing that once you have moved into the spiritual you will miss the physical desires; the physical needs; the physical joys; the simple things also of living, dancing, singing, just being and feeling the sun on your skin."

Tarra: - 'Yes . . . . Yes."

Venus: - *"To hold a perfect balance in these things is to see the illusion that you are neither spiritual nor physical but all of these things. That the physical is what you perceive as now and those feelings are very real. It is ok to be in the physical while enjoying the spiritual at the same time and you will not be stolen away by the spiritual nor held back by the physical. Does this make sense to you?"*

Tarra: - "It does. Yes, it does. I once described to a friend what I felt being with the twin flame was like. Now, I don't even know that there is such a thing but I can remember or . . . I seem to have a memory of . . . the passion and the love that that inspired and how my heart chakra opened to that. And I was . . . sort of compelled to open my friend's heart chakra (with her permission) for her to feel that, which she had never felt . . . at least in this life before. And it seems to be a memory of mine."

Venus: - *"Yes indeed the heart chakra is one of the most powerful chakras in the body because more often this is what is closed. We feel we are, loving others but more . . . it is unbalanced love. We are not receiving back so we then close the heart to protect ourselves. So when the heart chakra is opened it can be quite a physical, mental, emotional and spiritual shock to the whole body on all of these levels.*

Now I would like to say . . . as to twin flames . . . that the twin flame exists also as yourself because, as you are aware, all is one."

Tarra: - "Yes."

Venus: - "Meeting your twin flame is truly meeting your 'self', for some this may still involve some disconnection and they may perceive this as another, for others it is the true reconnection of the self."

Tarra: - Yes, and I think that's me.

Venus: - "You are truly correct in this."

Tarra: - "Mmm, I had an insight into that in reading a channel and it was sort of . . . such a disappointment to find out it was only me."

Venus: - "How could you be disappointed with only you? Only you encompass the entire Universe."

Tarra: - "I know but that's not how it seems from here."

Venus: - "In the true reconnection, with your twin flame, you'll feel a love like none other. You have been given a precious glimpse of this."

Tarra: - "Yes."

Venus: - "It will feel beyond words and you will not feel any lack at that time, believe me. You are experiencing this more and more. This feeling of knowing that you are completely satisfied with your 'Self' and I'm sure you can hear the capital in that."

Tarra: - "Yes I can."

Venus: - "When you are completely satisfied in yourself and feeling that connection with self, not necessarily the fireworks connection with self . . . that, you may take a little longer to truly experience, you will feel and draw towards you . . . the love – unconditional; passion – fiery;

and inspiration of others. People will be drawn to you like moths to a flame because you, by connecting to yourself, have connected to them because they are also your self."

Tarra: - "Mmm, uh ha, OK." (My brain became a pretzel about then.)

Venus: - "This seems too large to take in when all around you, you see individuals."

Tarra: - "Yes, it's . . . umm . . . upside down." (Laughing)

Venus: - (Joining in the laughter) "And this is only to be expected because at this time you are mainly in the physical trying to adjust to the spiritual that is coming in stronger and stronger. But, while you are here in the physical, you must maintain that balance."

Tarra: - "Yes."

Venus: - "But the veil grows thinner and thinner and truly it is up to you how much of the illusion you are comfortable in maintaining to have joy in this life. If you wish you can thin the veil so that you can see all things. All beings are one now however, if you feel more comfortable . . . in perceiving the physical; perceiving different personalities and archetypes. If you are comfortable with what you see around you . . . the sceneries; the environment; then that is beautiful and is perfect for you at this time. So many take unbelievable amounts of lives to see beyond the illusion largely because they choose to see the physical; it is purely your choice. It will not be stolen away from you. The illusion is not so much a lie as a beautiful thing created to bring comfort and joy . . . that gets twisted by our perspectives of lack and fear."

Tarra: - "Mmm, yes . . ."

Venus: - "So too the story of Adam and Eve in Eden . . . a beautiful place with all their needs provided for until they were told they had wisdom from the apple then they could see. Then they had trouble in assimilating because it brought in fear because they were concerned that their wisdom perhaps superseded Gods. That by being wise they were taking from God. Now we can tell you that this is not possible because you are one with God."

Tarra: - "That perception is still within our society to a large extent . . . not necessarily what people put on themselves but . . . the way they project outward on others if others show signs of reconnecting."

Venus: - "Yes."

Tarra: - "And I deal with it all the time but I don't know that I'm dealing with it, or think I'm dealing with it, in terms of my perception of what I'm seeing or feeling from others. Does that make sense?"

Venus: - "Perfectly . . . oftentimes as you know it is a mirror, what you are seeing . . . other times it is truly a disconnection between the others. For they are looking at you and seeing what they do not have and sometimes you are looking at them and seeing what you do not have."

Tarra: - "Yes."

Venus: - "Again, this is the illusion of the disconnection however this is also where people often feel ego arise when a student starts to succeed where they have not. Again, it's this perception of God that the student of God can never be stronger than God the teacher. Again the disconnection, there is no separation between God the teacher and God the student. We are all one, even those of us who have ascended; those of us who have been created as the pantheon we are all of the same flesh, the same blood, the same spirit. You have our wisdom deep inside you that you can call on at any time because it is your wisdom."

Tarra: - "Yes. I sort of . . . I understand that in some ways and sometimes I think oh, I'm being a Smart Alec here I'm pretending this is my wisdom when its spirits. Sometimes I get that as well in my perception so at those times I obviously don't understand that."

Venus: - "This is simply fears, fears that are awoken by the ego . . . because you are afraid that if you had this wisdom within you then you have no excuses for the mistakes and errors that you make along the way."

Tarra: - (That broke me up) "That's not nice being that perceptive."

Venus: - "Of course (trying not to laugh but barely succeeding) we know that all mistakes and errors are truly just another step along the path to enlightenment. So there's no need to fear."

Tarra: - "Yes, I know it's the responsibility that is the key."

Venus: - "Exactly, you have hit the nail on the head once more, oh wise one."

Tarra: - "So as long as you admit that you don't have that yet you can . . . you can stumble along." (Denial is a fool's tool but many of us use it from time to time. I didn't get much of a bite from making that statement.)

Venus: - "Oh but you do have responsibility – this is it, many people would prefer to believe in a God who sits above us on his throne making all decisions good and bad, that denial of responsibility in their own lives. That they have someone else to blame no matter what happens in their own lives they can blame it on God."

Tarra: - "Yes, well I don't do that. I must admit I used to argue before but I don't do that now – well I don't think I do."

Venus: - "Of course it's understandable because the majority of souls are not aware that they are living on more than one level. How for instance could an average soul believe that they could have created the disasters that happened across the world? If they were to believe this, this would set up the ego's guilt level for they would hold guilt for that and believe this to be a negative thing."

Tarra: - "Yes."

Venus: - "The average soul would not be able to take on the enormity of the understanding of realizing that in creating all things in our lives, we are creating balance and that there is a reason for everything as trite as that may sound."

Tarra: - "Yes, it does."

Venus: - "It is impossible for a natural disaster to occur somewhere on the world without it balancing the natural systems of the earth on all levels. It would not occur if this balance did not need to be created through the use of this natural disaster."

Tarra: - "Yes."

Venus: - "The same will also occur on a smaller scale in your own life for instance, as you know well, you may be traveling somewhere only to be diverted from your course. At first this brings up frustration as you look at your watch and feel impatience and anger because it is thwarting you from your purpose. Then later you discover that the reason for that diversion was a car accident that would have occurred at the same time that you were driving through the area."

Tarra: - "You're talking about an actual incident . . . are you? Or just a . . . "(I outline one such incident in Chapter 4.)

Venus: - "This incident has occurred many times throughout your life, Tarra."

Tarra: - "Oh yes, I get lost many times . . . or diverted."

Venus: - "Everybody is quite easily diverted because this is what the ego wishes, to keep the separation, to keep the responsibility onto others. The responsibility does not weigh nearly as heavily as most on earth believe. Response means to respond to something that occurs in you life. Ability means the abilities and strengths that you have already. Instead most . . . humans shall I say . . . think instead that a responsibility is a burden that others have put onto them when instead, a responsibility is in response to somebody else that you are well able to take care of with the abilities that you have."

Tarra: - "Yes, yes, and I find when I get out of being anxious and into knowing I don't have trouble with doing that. I get anxious for example when the e-mails were waiting for me when I got home the other day."

Venus: - "That's completely correct. Any time you are faced with the responsibility, and by you I mean all as one appearing as separate entities, every single being sees a responsibility on them 'selves' as a burden. So when you saw those e-mails you were faced with the need to respond using your abilities but you felt the weight of this because you did not want to let anybody else down and this is what impacts on most beings. They are afraid that a responsibility will lead to them letting down somebody else because they will not have the strength required to respond."

Tarra: - "Yes, anyway I did have it."

Venus: - "Of course you did. Just like you have untold healing abilities and these abilities that you have seen thus far are simply the tip of the iceberg."

Tarra: - "This thing I do know . . . I do know that. I do know that there's more to what I know than I'm letting myself see."

Venus: - "These are small fears but they feel big because again you are afraid that the stronger your abilities become the more responsibility you will hold towards those that you heal."

Tarra: - "Yes, I did feel last time when I had someone come to me for the Reconnective Healing, I did wonder if I was giving her of myself enough and of course that would have weakened it."

Venus: - "You did a splendid job at that time, it however, would have been clearer had you let go more and searched less. But you know this and that person came to you at that time because that was all they were ready for."

Tarra: - "Yes, but she also gave me a message from all of you I think, with the 'Crimson Circle' website."

Venus: - "Of course, there are no coincidences."

Tarra: - "Yes I was grateful, thank you."

Venus: - "I see you . . . I see you as the Priestess that you were at my temple."

Tarra: - "Oh, ok . . . (flustered and surprised at the unexpected change of subject) . . . do I know about this; is that to do with the Priestess Yve?"

Venus: - "This is a life that you have yet to explore but you will and you will do it alone. It was by the sea and you had golden ringlets and a love of animals that you have carried through to this life. I will say only this – that you put the noses of the priests out of joint."

Tarra: - "I seem to do that all the time, even now."

Venus: - "It is allowed because the male energy needs a jolt every now and again because it then puts them in their feminine energy because they feel nonplussed and hurt."

Tarra: - "Yes it's the hurt I don't like; the nonplussed is ok."

Venus: - "Oh, but the hurt is only to their ego,"

Tarra: - "Oh, ok. That's ok then."

Venus: - "It leaves them feeling vulnerable which puts them in their feminine energy. So every now and again a little knock doesn't do the male any harm."

Tarra: - "No."

Venus: - *"Also, as Mars hastens to remind me* (sounding amused), *often the females think they are the only ones who can nurture; the only ones who need attention."*

Tarra: - "Yes, I agree that we do think that sometimes. It's not true though."

Venus: - *"And when we are knocked by the males, who hasten to remind us this (stifled amusement), the female lioness comes out And of course the female lioness has lots of male energy so as the males knock us, thence comes the strong male energy. And when the females knock the males, comes the female energy and all is in balance once again."*

Tarra: - "Yes, yes . . . I was . . . I've had an interesting week doing the NSR course with Julie. Ah, it's . . . I think I'm just coming to terms with the fact that I seem to put peoples noses out of joint no matter . . . not always but, no matter where I am. I don't seem to . . . I don't know whether I meant to control it. I don't feel I'm meant to control it. I see myself push people away with the way I communicate. I don't seem to want to give up that method of communicating with people . . . or, is it bullying?"

Venus: - *"It is not bullying* (tape ends) . . . . (Missed a bit here I think) . . . (Flip side of tape) . . . . .*in this life. You are a powerful communicator. The things that you have to say are true and they seek deep for the soul of the person you are speaking to. However, often times when you speak you are also doing it, unaware, from a defensive level. Before even speaking you are afraid of how the person will take it."*

Tarra: - "Yes."

Venus: - *"And yet, you know the truth needs to be spoken so you often jump in boots and all as the expression is."*

Tarra: - "Yes, well some of my friends like that."

Venus: - "That is true, and that is why you are the one who is called to speak to so many. However you need only to check your heart chakra to know whether the person you are speaking to at the time . . . you need to come through the heart to speak. This does not mean that you need to speak in a false or light-hearted manner. It means only that you need to check through your heart and know that you are saying this for their highest 'self'."

Tarra: - "Yes."

Venus: - "99% of the time you are coming wholly from a place of spirit for this persons highest good but occasionally you are being asked by your ego to respond to something that you feel because of what somebody else has said. This is not very often but it can impact and impact on you more so than the person you are speaking to."

Tarra: - "Yes, particularly in credibility."

Venus: - "That's correct. So for your own integrity, for your own sense of power and truth, check only that you are speaking through the heart and all else will follow."

Tarra: - "I'll try to understand that (uncertain) sometimes I don't . . . although I understand the words and I understand what the instruction seems to mean, in practice I don't always understand it . . . you know . . . when I have to apply it."

Venus: - "You are not alone. If you understood everything that came through all the time you would no longer be here where you are now. And once again when you are ready, when you do understand all the little nuances, all the little sign posts that show that all is illusion, all is one and that you are the master creator then you will ascend but it will be your choice. This is not a responsibility that you can pass on to anybody else."

Tarra: - "No."

Venus: - *"Our God, our beloved God of whom you are part as am I, will not sit on a heavenly throne and reach his large white hand down and pluck you and draw you up."*

Tarra: - (Laughing) "Actually I don't think I've ever seen . . . envisioned that for myself."

Venus: - *"You will only be able to envision it with laughter now I'm sure as you can see it is your choice."*

Tarra: - "Mind you I did do a painting with it going the other way, baby through to childhood through to adult with the hand, I did do a painting like that."

Venus: - *"There does exist a figurative hand that guides us throughout time because if not, and this is known as the holy spirit to some . . . if not for the hand that shows itself in truly spiritual moments we would all exist in the abyss. In the separation because we would have no beacons of light to draw us home."*

Tarra: - "Mmm, true."

Venus: - *"Mars grows impatient and wishes to push me aside. He will have to wait a little longer. Let me embrace you sister. You're a shining light of womanhood on all levels."*

Tarra: - "Thank you. It's so wonderful to speak to you again. I know I keep everyone in . . . individual (as individuals) but it sort of keeps me with my friends when I do it that way."

Venus: - *"That's fine because if you didn't keep us individualized I wouldn't be here."*

Tarra: - "Ok, oh, you mean you'd go poof and you'd be gone."

Venus: - *"That is so, for we are creations of your soul."*

Tarra: - "Then I'll keep you individualized."

MARS

Mars: - "Beloved Tarra I am Mars

Tarra: - "Oh, hello . . ."

Mars: - and you are sexier than you will ever know."

(I wasn't expecting that and Caz and I broke into peals of laughter.)

Mars: - "Oh, is your blood tingling because mine is?"

Tarra: - (Getting a little pink here but laughing) "you'll embarrass me."

Mars: - "Venus is at this moment swatting me like a fly."

Tarra: - "I bet she is!"

Mars: - "She will keep. My energy is far more than sexual as you know."

Tarra: - "Yes."

Mars: - "It is about the passions of life, and of spirit, and of creativity, and of the moment of creation, and of the power that exists within you to create as well as to receive . . . for it is the feminine that receives and draws to you the energies to be able to create. Also does the physical perceive this, for in truth, as Venus has already so beautifully put it . . . oh, she's pretty isn't she? . . ."

Tarra: - (Laughing at his deliberately deep throated, sultry tone) "yes."

Mars: - "All is one but here on the earth so many opposites are perceived and too often the male and the female are seen as opposites instead of partners. Together we are all working on showing it as the partnership that, instead of on the opposing sides, you cannot do without the male or the female. You will see a manifestation of this in those perfectly interesting transsexuals and transvestites, particularly those who like to show themselves, who glory in their masculine form while dressing in the glamour of the female. Interestingly, as you know, in the animal kingdom it is the male that wears the brightest plumage anyway."

Tarra: - "Yes, yes it is. Well they'd have to otherwise we wouldn't be attracted would we?"

Mars: - "That's right because us males cannot help ourselves but want to be attractive. And for all a male may complain about how long it takes a female in front of the mirror it is usually the male who spends more time obsessing with their physical characteristic."

Tarra: - "Really? Well I know they take longer in a fitting room when they're buying clothes."

Mars: - "Oh, now we wouldn't want some areas to be too snug and not give us air would we?"

Tarra: - (Peals of appreciative laughter at that from Caz and I. He was sounding so prim.) "No."

Mars: - "And, males can not help but be pyromaniacs . . . because we like to set things alight, including males themselves. This is why they are so interested in sports and anything that brings an adrenalin rush because it sets them alight."

Tarra: - "True and it's about the only area, in the western society really, where they can touch male to male."

Mars: - "Ah ha, not 'just a pretty face' are we Tarra."

Tarra: - "No."

Mars: - "You see what is (the) *truth. That throughout history males have needed a physical outlet and in the current climate, in the western world at least, there are very little physical outlets that do not involve sports of some kind."*

Tarra: - "No."

Mars: - "For many men they are not confident enough to get up off their couches and do the physical themselves, which is a shame, their feminine sides . . . their negative feminine sides . . . are telling them that they are not good enough; not strong enough. Does this make sense?"

Tarra: - "Yes, I've actually done that to someone. I've said something like that to K at one point but not . . . not like that . . . it was more to do with being a male character; letting the character be strong. So it was not nice."

Mars: - "That's right. Again that battle of the sexes comes into play and interestingly enough, when a female is battling a male for supremacy, she is bringing out her male side without even seeking for it."

Tarra: - "Yes."

Mars: - "And when a male whines that his needs are not being taken care of he's bringing in the negative female; just as the woman by trying to stand over the male and assert herself, is showing the negative male."

Tarra: - "Yes well I understand that now, possibly I didn't then."

Mars: - "And may I just say that on the physical level this is why the allure of the 69 is so fascinating even though so many fear to do it and don't really feel comfortable at the time . . ."

Tarra: - "Yes, yes (Embarrassed and hoping this subject will go away although interested nonetheless)."

Mars: - ". . . because truly, at heart neither wants to be dominated by the other nor dominate the other."

Tarra: - "Yes, ok I understand that. (Bright red by now wishing I didn't have to face this.) That makes sense." (Things personal to another omitted.)

Mars: - "In fact, it is probably one of the most balanced sexual acts. Unfortunately, for many, they are afraid to be so vulnerable because in truth it is also the most vulnerable of the sexual acts."

Tarra: - "Yes, it is."

Mars: - "And I bring this up, not to be a dirty old man . . ."

Tarra: - (I couldn't help it, I broke up again which I think is what he wanted to relieve my embarrassment) "Really?"

Mars: - ". . . but to show some symbolism."

Tarra: - "Of the circle . . . ?"

Mars: - "In fact, yes. The circles the male and the female is shown in the 69, it is also reflected in the sign of the crab; the sign of cancer."

Tarra: - "Yes um, I understand the symbol of the 69 but the crab I'm not familiar with . . . not consciously familiar with."

Mars: - "The cancer symbol is a 69 sideways."

Tarra: - "Ah ha . . ." (Of course it is – duh.)

Mars: - "And to bring this even closer and stronger perspective cancer itself, the disease which is in fact a name for many diseases, shows itself most predominately at this time in breast and prostrate cancer."

Tarra: - "Yes."

Mars: - "There are of course many other kinds of cancers but these ones in particular are showing themselves more and more often because of the imbalance of the male and female. I'm sure you can see the correlations."

Tarra: - "Yes I can."

Mars: - "More and more often those who find themselves with these cancers are forced to look at their own sexuality and to bring into balance those parts of themselves they feel are missing. Those who are able to do this are more often than not healed and go on to teach others. Then of course there are those who are able to who then choose to leave."

Tarra: - "Yes, ok, by dying with cancer you mean . . . still?"

Mars: - "Yes however, in most cases, those who linger on longer and more painfully are those still seeking the answers."

Tarra: - "Yes, ok. Ah, so much . . . there's just so much that needs to fall into place for me. I know it's all there within me . . . just allowing it out. But, one of the things I did learn from last week is that a lot of the things that I thought were blocks weren't necessarily so but just habit in the way I perceive; in the way I do things; in the way I react to things (a personal realization that had been hovering just beyond my reach for years). It's just habit to hurt, rather than actually needing to respond to that anymore."

Mars: - "That's right, habits; dirty little habits; nasty long-term habits; they all come from laziness in truth."

Tarra: - "Right . . . (but, not really wanting to accept that)"

Mars: - "Where you are stuck in a rut and it is much easier to react in a way that has become ingrained than to search for the truth in every situation . . . because you feel that to do so would take far too much effort, too much time . . . forgetting of course that time can be expanded to fit your needs."

Tarra: - "Yes, well I don't always remember that, no."

Mars: - "No, it's a bit hard for that to be remembered when everywhere in the human world there are clocks and watches."

Tarra: - "I should be able to do that at the moment now . . . because I've pulled myself away from that. I don't even remember to listen to the news let alone anything else . . . and the only reason I really go to bed is because I get tired so, I should be able to manage that. I think you're right, it's possibly just laziness but one of the things I also find, and advise of this too, is that it's more the beginning than the actually doing and . . . in change or with anything . . . and I advise people that this is the case. That this is the block not the actual doing and I don't follow my own advice."

Mars: - "Very few of us do. For instance I, who preach of the need for balance between the male and female, enjoy being male."

Tarra: - "Yes, well, so you should. Shouldn't you?"

Mars: - "Yes, I have of course my feminine side and she's standing beside me because we are two halves of a whole. Just like you seem to be a fragment of a whole but are indeed the whole also. Are you confused yet?"

Tarra: - "Not really. No, not really because I do feel because I don't know myself totally . . . consciously I mean . . ."

Mars: - "You know yourself better than you think you do . . . (laughing) . . . and we heard the crowds roar approval because they knew you were not confused because you are able to grasp quite easily, random thoughts and make sense of them where others may not . . ."

Tarra: - (Gleeful laughter) . . . "Yes" . . . (I had forgotten about the crowds who are always present on the other side listening in to the teachings of the Masters and to gain an understanding of human life.)

Mars: - . . . and you do not give yourself enough credit for this or for the forces of creation that are present in your life."

Tarra: - "Um, forces of creation? Like you for example, do you mean? (We then said together) *"No, in your own 'self'"* "No, in my 'self' you mean?"

Mars: - "Your own ability to create and manifest the things in your life which you have so often done, you easily forget."

Tarra: - "Ok, yes."

Mars: - "A suggestion at this time, if you are not journaling already, is to do this more often and clearly show the things that you have actually physically done during the day as well as what you have been thinking."

Tarra: - "Yes I haven't done that. Well, sometimes I do that to let myself know what I have achieved. That I haven't been wasting time on a human or spiritual level . . . sometimes I actually do that to see. It gives me a sort of perspective of where I've been and where I'm going. Sometimes I do that."

Mars: - "Now Tarra, its time for Venus and I to go but I just wanted you to know that your all powerful, St. Michael the Archangel is still present with you; looking over you – that transsexual dream. (Mars sounded very amused) *by this, of course I mean that there are plenty of males out there who would wish to look exactly as Michael does in the hearts and minds of all the females that he comes into contact with."*

Tarra: - "Yes oh well, mine's much more beautiful and stronger than anyone else's perception of him."

Mars: - "Ah, I'm jealous!"

(Peals of gleeful, uncontrolled laughter from Caz and me)

Mars: - "As Mars of course some people see me as a quite scary figure or as simply a big red planet."

Tarra: - (As we channel, I often have visions of those I'm speaking to. All I was able to see of Mars was this large, muscley, hairy red chest. Just as well I should think given some of our explicit conversation.) "I've been trying to picture you, I just haven't thought of you in a physical . . . (rather tongue tied) . . . no that's not what I want to say . . . human type figure. I imagine you to be quite . . . no my history is not quite good enough. I can see . . . (digging a hole for myself here as I tried to be honest and flatter at the same time) muscley, very big muscley person (I couldn't stop laughing)."

Mars: - "I'm liking you more and more."

Tarra: - "But that might not be what Venus wants?"

Mars: - "I have my visions of her too and she is sometimes dressed more scantily than she would wish."

Tarra: - (Both Caz and I are practically rolling around on the floor with laughter at this point.) "Last time I saw her she was in black leather."

Mars: - "Yes."

Tarra: - "Do you wear leather too?"

Mars: - "(A very deep sexy) Yeeeees. Perhaps a name I could give you that would also clearly help you is Backus."

Tarra: - "Yes, well I'll have to look that up because obviously that is 'in Caz's understanding' and not mine. Thank you."

Mars: - "Farewell Tarra, remember that together we are all working towards the female and male balance and that you have a wonderful balance of both."

Tarra: - "I can feel that, thank you for coming."

Mars: - "Oh! Let me embrace you too."

Tarra: - "Oh yes, yes, yes thank you."

Caz: - ". . . . . *That was a bit of a ride! (*We couldn't stop laughing.*)*"

8 June, 2006

RAGOU (I have spelt his name as he pronounced it)

Caz: - "Ok, this is interesting I'm getting pictures of the Sudan and they're calling it that – the Sudan. . . . . . . And your there as you are now"

Tarra: - "Oh, ok."

Caz: - "Interesting . . . . all I can see at the moment is like . . . just like someone just taking pictures of you there and little children coming up and calling you by name. I'm being shown these things but I don't know . . . it feels like there are people there but I'm not getting any sensation of who so, if you wanted to ask anything you can just go for it and see what comes up."

Tarra: - "Well yes, I'm just feeling the sensations at the back of my head which feels like I can feel every part of my brain."

Caz: - "Yes, I can feel like we are surrounded by a circle of people at the moment but I don't know."

Tarra: - "Is it the group I work with then?"

Caz: - "I'm getting a 'yes' on that one."

Tarra: - "Are they meaning I'm working there energetically, really?"

Caz: - "Yes, yes. They all look very similar and yet different; they're all about the same age as you so they must have entered at the same time "

Tarra: - "Right, well I'm really pleased to understand that I'm doing something somewhere and I'm very aware of the different levels of consciousness and the energy . . . that obviously must be working in all different places . . . just not conscious of it." (By that I mean I don't remember details)

Caz: - "There's a Sudanese man here and his name is Ragou."

Tarra: - "I don't know Ragou, hello Ragou."

Caz: - "(whispering inaudibly)"

Tarra: - "Hmm, you're whispering."

*Caz: - "Ok, he wants me to interpret because he doesn't speak the language. He's saying that **"He's with you and you're with him; that he's Sudanese".**"*

Tarra: - "We're together energetically?"

Caz: - "Yes, as are all of these people, he's gesturing to them and they are all nodding their heads. Everyone's joined holding hands and it's like you're in the center but you're also in the circle. They are all there but not there . . . it's like I'm getting pictures of them in different places at the same time."

Tarra: - "So, we obviously work with the children of the Sudan energetically, as a group, together."

*Caz: - "He's telling me that **"There have been different ones who've been called to go there physically as well and this choice is available to you as well should you ever decide to take it but that you're working there energetically now."** And very, very strongly it's like you're there."*

Tarra: - "Right, that's very good. I'm becoming more aware of allowing things to happen and . . . it would be nice to be conscious of these things but I don't think I'm emotionally mature enough to be conscious of these things yet or spiritually even . . . mature enough." (When transcribing this, I am very surprised to see that I actually thought that way – what a circumstance to manifest for myself.)

Caz: - "He's shaking his head. Ok he said he's going to put his energy into speaking."

Ragou: - "Tarra, you must understand there is no maturity or immaturity there is just being."

Tarra: - "Ok, I'm beginning to . . . when people point things out to me and spirit points things out to me . . . I'm beginning to grasp the concepts a bit better now."

Ragou: - "Every time you consider yourself as being not where you want to be, or as you put it not there yet, you are denying yourself and your own abilities. You are spirit; you are with us; you just are; you do not need to question at what level, what stage or whether you are doing enough."

Caz: "Ah, he's laughing . . . he's trying to find the words."

Ragou: - "Sometimes you think you are, as Aussies say, 'slacking off'. This is not the case, just 'chill out'; to just be and as you do this you will get more pictures of your work on other levels . . . stronger sensations. It is you who have denied yourself these things."

Tarra: - "Yes well I understand that that's the case well, I'm sorry . . . theoretically I understand that that's the case. I'm not able . . . not unable to accept . . . I just don't know it as the case from my human perspective or from my perspective at all – this consciousness."

Caz: - "He understands this; he's shaking his head though, he says . . ."

Ragou: - "There's no apologies needed; you cannot apologize for all of the work that you are doing on all of these levels while still feeling uncertain you are still feeling trusting enough to put yourself out there."

Tarra: - "Yes, yes I had lost for a little while that feeling of the expansion of my being or actually feeling myself expanding but I think that I'm getting that back again now with a little bit more understanding."

Caz: - "He is saying that like him . . ."

Ragou: - "You need to remember that you are as one and to feel that you are surrounded by other loving energies; those . . . the same as you here for the same reason as well as those from other dimensions . . . entities. You cannot deny that you are a part of this but that you are constantly denying it by questioning yourself. There is nothing wrong with questioning others but too much questioning of yourself takes you away from spirit."

Tarra: - "Yes, I think I've begun to understand that and I've also begun to understand that in doing that also . . . . I isolate myself. Probably, on a sub-conscious level that's deliberate because I had been saying that once I do know consciously about things I'm afraid that I can't maintain what I begin. But, I understand that the other aspects, or the way I think of it as other aspects or other dimensions, do understand."

Caz slips into trance channel.

Ragou: - "Yes but it is like denying yourself. Denying your right to be yourself, always seem to be comparing yourself, feeling less and this is also denying others because you are one. All of these people here in this circle have moments of denial but their heart tells them they must still work; work in all these energies. They know that they are part of the circle just as they know they need to breathe physically. There is no denying they are one with all and yet daily they do."

Tarra: - "It's a human trait, I guess."

Ragou: - "In the Sudan we have no time for self-recrimination or the observing of the self. Survival is all."

Tarra: - "Yes, I understand . . . I understand that and I know. I had been discussing my situation with Caz in that I've chosen a very luxurious way of having a lower vibrational existence in this experience."

Ragou: - *"You can tell yourself that as many times as you like; it is not true and you know this."*

Tarra: - "What . . . that it's a luxurious way?"

Ragou: - *"That there is any vibrational level but that which is."*

Tarra: - "Ok, well I'm not sure I understand that."

Ragou: - *"No, and you do not need to seek to understand but to just be."*

Tarra: - "Ok."

Ragou: - *"The best way to take oneself out of the mind and into the heart and into the being is to busy oneself and to busy oneself outside of oneself. Working with others for others stops the mind from seeking to distract itself from being one. As I said, here in the Sudan, we have no time for self-recrimination for asking many questions that takes oneself away from all that is because we are often purely in the physical and spiritual. We must eat or we die. It is our spiritual songs, our rhythms that keep us truly alive. I must advise that more music in your life, more physical doing in your life, will help you take you out of your mind but you know this."*

Tarra: - "Yes, I also know that if I . . . . Yes, you know what I'm thinking yes . . . . There's something that stops me."

Ragou: - *"Oftentimes Tarra you deny yourself and deny your role in this world. You often believe that you are not welcomed by others. This is a belief you have. This is not the belief of others but by having this belief you reflect this onto others and thus manifest it. There is no time for these self-recriminations. You must live each moment outside of yourself being one with all instead of separating yourself. This is not to say that you must never spend time alone but to be aware that there is truly no such thing as being alone. And again you tell yourself that you are destined to spend the rest of your life alone but this is impossible."*

Tarra: - "Not so much alone . . . I'm talking about the physical life . . . I just feel that if I don't get close, too close, to a particular person then I won't have problems with communication and stuff like that . . . that's all . . . maintaining it."

Ragou: - "I think sometimes the words fear and feel are very close together."

Tarra: - "Yes, very possibly . . ."

Ragou: - "Inside the strongest emotion that drives your life is 'What about me?' This is not to say that you have any selfishness."

Caz: - (Suddenly popping out of the trance channel) "There's somebody else coming in on that – a female energy. Ragou's standing aside."

This is the first and only time while working with Caz that she popped in and out of the trance channel like this but we both took it in our stride. With a deep breath she went back into the trance.

In this portion of the channel is my core reason for writing this book. It surprises me with the raw emotion it brings up in me even now. Quan Yin felt my annoyance building at the way the discussion with Ragou was going. She had been pushing my buttons.

QUAN YIN

Quan Yin: - "This is Quan Yin."

Tarra: - "Hello, Quan Yin. Is Ragou still there?"

Quan Yin: - "Yes we are one."

Tarra: - "Oh lovely, thank you Ragou . . ."

Quan Yin: - "My words through him and now I stand aside. Ah Tarra, Tarra it is well that all beings say 'What about me?' because in that one statement there are many questions. 'What am I meant to be doing?' 'What better could I be doing?' 'Am I good enough; am I worthy enough?' Beloved there is nothing wrong with this question."

Tarra: - "I lost the train (of thought) . . . I wanted to say something to you about that. It's not . . . for all of you, it's not that I don't necessarily want to do anything and I know that I get into conflict where I get isolated or I feel isolated when I get involved with a lot of people. So, for example, working . . . I had been thinking . . . (I had to back track here). There's a group that was mentioned to me when I was at a second-hand furniture shop in Toowoomba. The guy was going over to work with this group (Fred Hollows Foundation) and I thought that would be a really good thing to do. But, imagine if I got to another country where I was . . . well I've lived in other countries before . . . but where I got to a country where through communicating inadequately I isolated myself from the locals then it would be a very hard way to live."

Quan Yin: - "So you realize dear heart what your fear is?"

Tarra: - "Yes I know what my fear is."

Quan Yin: - "Tell me."

Tarra: - "Well it's just fear."

Quan Yin: - "Fear of what . . . ?"

Tarra: - God I hate doing this and I hate how it makes me feel to have someone, anyone, delve into my psyche like this, invading my privacy in this way. "Well . . . communicating; not communicating correctly; not being able to communicate."

Quan Yin: - "Deeper dear heart, what does your fear of not being able to communicate your feelings lead to; what is the worst that could happen?"

Tarra: - "Well . . . isolation I guess."

Quan Yin: - "That is correct; your deepest fear is isolation. Why might you have that?"

Tarra: - "I don't know."

Quan Yin: - "Could it be, in the falsity of the separation from spirit, that you most fear not being able to reconnect being left to drift?"

Tarra: - "True, yes in a way but by the same token I'm a bit afraid to reconnect if it means . . . I have a bit of difficulty understanding a conglomerate; a whole; the one . . . where it feels like you lose your mind to everything else."

Quan Yin: - "By saying this you are saying that you fear losing yourself and you fear losing your identity to the one."

Tarra: - "Yes."

Quan Yin: - "But you are the one."

Tarra: - "Yes but I don't understand that because I don't think the way everyone else does. I don't think I think the way Saint Germaine would or Kuthumi or Indira Ghandi or Michael. I don't feel that I think the same."

Quan Yin: - "But there is no thought, all is a creation."

Tarra: - Quan Yin is the gentlest soul however by this time I was feeling totally exposed and vulnerable but I had to learn, after all that is why I'm doing this. "Well then obviously I don't know the one."

Quan Yin: - "You can only use the tools that you believe you have Tarra and throughout this life your pattern has been fear of isolation yet fear of being absorbed into the whole."

Tarra: - "Yes." Monosyllabic answers now while trying to ease the pain

Quan Yin: - "This is like somebody stranded on a desert island for many decades they fear being alone for all eternity but they are just as afraid of what they will say and how they will be embraced if they return to society. That fear encompasses whether society comes to them; seeks them out or whether they seek out society. You feel that the only way you can work with groups is if you feel ready to embrace them and they feel ready to embrace you, but as you, with no changes to yourself and this is wonderful because this is understandable. However oftentimes, you imagine that all those others seek to change you instead of truly embracing who you are."

Tarra: - "That's true."

Quan Yin: - "You need to worry less about what others expectations and beliefs are about you and just be and as those fears and worries lift so will your heart and you will see that you are worthy. You are doing great works on many levels and on many levels you are working with others. Your real struggle at this time is with the physical. You have locked yourself, you believe, into the physical. You are not perceiving the other levels because you are focusing only on the physical and seeing getting to the other levels as a struggle; as you not being worthy. Any time you cannot recall the work you do in your sleep or on other levels you berate yourself. You think you are not working hard enough. You are not giving up of yourself enough. It is always you, you feel you are not doing enough nobody else is telling you this."

Tarra: - "True."

Quan Yin: - "Yet here you are working on these other levels with all these others and I can tell you now that you are not the only one of these people, of these souls, that is having the difficulties you are having with

perceiving your oneness. It is not Tarra, as part of you believes, that you are the one trailing behind. That you are the one being carried by these others; that you are struggling to keep up. You are as worthy as all others. There is nobody judging you but yourself."

Tarra: - "I'm pleased to hear I'm not dragging people back or souls back."

Quan Yin: - "Oh Tarra, what are we going to do with you? Just as you are afraid of giving up of yourself to others my dear you are also afraid of hurting them and holding them back as you are afraid of them doing this to you. You see this ever turning circle of struggle?"

Tarra: - "Yes."

Quan Yin: - "But, it is understandable my dear for you to have these fears of hurting and being hurt and of giving up of yourself because of your youth, of your childhood, of your womanhood; that constant circle of giving up of yourself to others and feeling that you have not received the same courtesy. It is not that you have been feeling that you deserve more; that you are being treated not as well as you deserve but more that you feel secretly that you must not be worthy of others true deep and abiding love, companionship and trust. That this is something that would have to be earned by you giving more perhaps than them; this has become a pattern for you."

Tarra: - "Mmm, well I'll break that pattern."

Quan Yin: - "That sounds quite determined."

Tarra: - "Yes . . . if I find a way through then I will try to use it."

Quan Yin: - "I would like you to say 'I will find a way through'."

Tarra: - "I will find a way through."

Quan Yin: - "This is up to you to clear but please be aware this is not only you having this struggle. This is quite a universal struggle particularly for those who do lightwork."

Tarra: - "Yes, I think I have understood that as well. Yes, I have understood that."

Quan Yin: - "This is why my major mission, while working with the light, is compassion. You must have compassion for yourself and your journey back to the oneness. You have not been abandoned, you have never left, this separation is your perception but do not beat yourself up for this. You are not alone in these fears so too, as you know how you feel, have compassion for those others who have the same fears which is indeed every soul on earth."

Tarra: - "Yes, I think I've understood this . . . I think I also understand . . . (personal to another) . . . sort of taking the emphasis and placing it directly on the soul as the life rather than the physical. Working from where I'm conscious . . . and understanding that really I need to be working from the soul perspective, not the level but the perspective. This would make it much clearer and easier to find the way I think."

Quan Yin: - "That is true and it is correct however that is also questioning of your 'self'. To just be is not to question but just to feel from the heart and respond as it guides you. If you feel anger in your heart and you need to release it then do so; if you feel joy then do so; if you feel the need to be with others then do so; and when you feel the need to be by yourself, well you know, do so. This is the way to awakening; this is the way to ascension to just be and I hear the words of many who may see this perspective as a cop out."

Tarra: - "Yes. It sort of . . . um . . . brings up an image of a blank canvas."

Quan Yin: - "A blank canvas is the most terrifying thing of all and yet it is the most beautiful because it is white and clear and pure. An artist or those who do not believe themselves to be artists are intimidated and excited by this nothingness, this blank canvas and now you see why."

Tarra: - "Yes."

Quan Yin: - "It is the not knowing that is exciting when you unwrap your presents on a Christmas morning. It is the not knowing that makes a day exciting as the sun peeks over the horizon. To know all is to have no joy and no excitement in the living, in the moment and yet humans seek always to know as some kind of security blanket."

Tarra: - "Yes, I think I realize what you are going to say even before I speak but . . . I've been trying to free my life up so that I don't have these complications. But of course again . . . I still think of maintaining the physical being and jumping into the unknown is still a difficult thing. Even if I decide to go to the Sudan or somewhere . . . where I've had thoughts about going and helping in other places or being in other places . . . my conscious knowledge of how to do that is just not there either. I feel uncomfortable about searching it out but when I'm ready, I will."

Quan Yin: - "Like an artist with a blank canvas the ideas flit through the mind but which one should one invest one's time and energy in? If one puts brush to canvas has one chosen the right colour? Is the brush in the right position? Should one be using a brush at all? These are the questions that always face all of us as we take steps into the unknown but when an artist is in the moment his instincts will pick up the right brush, the right colour without conscious thought and it will flow. The energy takes over and there is no thought, of food or water or material possessions or comfort as the energy flows onto the blank canvas, until suddenly the canvas is alive with colour and passion and warmth and expression and emotion and spirit. It is fear that gets between all souls and their return to oneness. Please do not be so hard on yourself. Your life at this moment is a blank canvas. You have many tools available to you but as yet the passion, the excitement has not hit you to begin work."

Tarra: -"No."

Quan Yin: - "You have simply been preparing the equipment you need and like all artists their rising excitement, their energy that is available even when they do not have an idea to work with, inspires those around them and this is you Tarra. Your energy inspires others."

Tarra: - "Yes I've seen that happening (Point personal to another omitted)."

Quan Yin: - "It is all the little things that we do not look at that are important . . . as simple as growing a belief in oneself. This is how you help others by showing them that you are human like they are that we are all seeking and will find. My path was not always an easy one. It is not necessarily easy now . . . (time weary big sigh) . . . as I struggle to convince you of your own self-worth but beloved heart it is what I do, so I must continue."

Tarra: - (Laughing sympathetically at her frustration) "Yes."

Quan Yin: - "It is what I am driven to do to bring you back to wholeness; to have compassion for yourself; to forgive yourself and those around you who led you to where you are at this moment. A blank canvas is an exciting thing to have but if the artist fears to take the step of picking up the brush its destiny will never be fulfilled. Your greatest fear is in picking up the wrong brush."

Tarra: - "Yes, however . . . . ."

Quan Yin: - "However, my spirit will help you to find the right brush at the right time in the right place."

Tarra: - "Yes, thank you."

Quan Yin: - "I know you are feeling this right now, this sense of oneness. Feel all those around you feel their heartbeat feel their lungs expand with air. Feel this pulse of the heartbeat and the breath all around you . . . there is no separation. There is no need to question it is just there, you have focus on your heart dear heart. At any time you feel yourself feeling lonely or fearful, when you are terrified of where the next step will take you to; when you feel emptiness, focus on that heart close your eyes see your heart expanding and red and pulsing.

Realize this is the same heart as all others, feel the breath of spirit, focus on this for a few moments. . . . . You are beautiful. All is beautiful it is only the fears that make things ugly. I need you to forgive yourself. I need you to hold your inner self, kiss its eyelids and give it your blessing. Together you have come a long way through pain and happiness but you are one and you have conquered yet another mountain together. Blessed be beautiful one."

Tarra: - "Thank you."

Quan Yin: - *"I'm with you always."*

Tarra: - "Yes, I know."

Ragou: - *"It is I Ragou. I'm touching your nose with my nose, my forehead to your forehead and clasping your hands. I am your brother, I am your sister."*

14 August, 2006

Leading up to the following session I had lost a friend through reacting with heightened sensitivity to something she said to me. This is quite common too for one who has low self-esteem which I thought I had gone past only to have it come back and kick me in the backside.

I did not realize that what I was experiencing was my heart opening up more and as a result normal feelings and emotions were intensified. I made a decision, one that I realized I would probably regret, that I would not continue with the sessions with the same degree of tenacity that I had in the past. The following was the teams answer to my decision.

THE TEAM

Caz: - ". . . . . I can feel a few here . . . the one that has come forward who I feel the most is Mother Mary. . . . ."

Tarra: - "I can feel . . . I don't know what it is . . . but in my head it feels really odd."

Caz: - "She was brushing the back of your head before."

Tarra: - "Was she?"

Caz: - "Keeping her hand on the back of your head."

Tarra: - "Mmm, I can feel that."

Caz: - "I don't know if she's stepping in or if she just wants me to speak for her. . . . ."

Tarra: - "Energies . . . . Is there anyone who wants to speak to me?"

Mother Mary: - "Beloved Tarra, it is I Mother Mary placing a kiss on your forehead and my hand on your heart and wiping a tear from your eye and kissing each of your eyelids. Now my forehead is against yours and my hands cupping the back of your head. I want you to breathe in this energy, feel the unconditional love . . . we have no expectations of you; we have no plans for you. These are your creations as are your fears, your desires, and your past. Please allow yourself to release your own expectations because your fear of not being able to meet these is what causes so many of your blockages towards living in the now and allowing your true skills and abilities to come through. You recall too, when you were very young, comments such as she won't amount to much; laughter tied with your name. All these little barbed comments from siblings, parents and family acquaintances stuck in your skin and made you feel uncomfortable within your skin . . . causing you to search outward to see your reflection in others. And yet, when you see yourself reflected, you discount the beauty and look only at what you perceive to be the ugly, you have forgotten all the loving comments. You tell yourself that you remember them but it is not these that stick in your skin and wound your heart. You know that there is only one opinion that counts – that is your own. If you always search in the reflection of others this will mean nothing. Feel my kiss feel my thumbs on your temples. Trust that there is nothing to fear in just being. Open the crown chakra, feel the insurgents of energies coming from throughout the Universe being funneled into your body, into your aura, into your chakras. See the grid lines of this funnel . . . this is how you take on the world. You pull in every . . . little insecurity and fear of others into your body hoping to heal them and through them yourself. This is a large part of the work you do and you are not giving yourself credit for it. You are too often allowing these energies to pollute yourself instead of being transmuted into the light. Allow the energies to funnel through you; see them instantly; be consumed by the light. Allow that energy to then pour into the earth, circle the heart this is part of what you naturally do. Often the energies get stuck because of your fears that you are not enough, that you don't have the abilities . . . create a blockage. I know it is easy for us to say just trust when you have had your fingers burnt but that is simply it. Trust that you have an enormous capacity for healing and being healed but this compassion that you have for all can be funneled like the energies into light instead of soaking up all the negative, all the fear all the anger and all the guilt, for unconsciously you draw these toward you seeking to heal them seeking to heal your own fears and angers. We implore you to find a ritual that you are comfortable with. Your own, your own creation to remind you that you are a conduit. That you can transmute the energies that you do not need to hold onto them, you do not need to direct them just simply allow them to be light. Come with me as we rise up already miles above the earth looking back down seeing the glow around the earth. See here the others with me the Archangels Michael, Uriel, Raphael, Gabriel, the legions behind them. You see to my right Lord Ashtar, Kuthumi and more. You see yourself standing between us no more, no less. Tarra, we are one. It is not your fault that you feel the separation . . . the separation is lifting. You are understanding it on deeper and deeper levels. You see us, you feel us and yes you hear us. As you are aware, you have created blockages towards these things, we've always been here and always been speaking to you. You have continually second guessed yourself, your communications, your abilities. We are here now to tell you that time is over. No more Tarra . . . no more excuses, no more separations. Feel our kisses each and every one of us as we take your head in our hands, touch our lips to your forehead, first . . . ."

Kuthumi: - "Kuthumi . . . beloved Tarra"

Tarra: - "Hello."

Kuthumi: - "It is as Mother Mary says, there is no separation. My forehead against your forehead - feel your third eye opening. There are no barriers . . . remember this."

Ashtar: - "Lord Ashtar . . . beloved Tarra"

Tarra: - "Hello."

Ashtar: - "Always and ever I am here above and within the earth as you are above, within, and on the earth. Never discount the work you do on the other plains."

Tarra: - "No, I don't think I do . . . I think I do here."

Ashtar: - "We are simply here to remind you there is no separation. Feel my kiss on your forehead . . . this is my pledge and my seal that your work is vital."

Michael: - "Archangel Michael – see how we have come to slap you around my dear."

Tarra: - (Laughing even when I didn't feel the least bit like laughing by this stage because I was trying to hold back my tears.) "Yes, well I've been slapping you around a lot."

Michael: - *"Feel my arms . . . my wings around you beloved Tarra, my kiss on your eyelids . . . my strength is yours. You are always and ever protected."*

Tarra: - "I know that."

Michael: - *"Ah, but often you like to think that you are left hanging out on a limb . . . we've all left you to hang out to dry so to speak."*

Tarra: - "No I don't think that, I just get angry because I can't see it."(which of course drives that ability away)

Michael: - *"It amuses me and saddens me at the same time to see you beat yourself up so. It is there always, your abilities and yet you always pass them on to others. Part of this however, is because one of your abilities is in strengthening others. Feel my forehead against yours, again feel my strength . . . it is yours. Remember you have the ability to pluck the daggers and swords that you allow to cover yourself – to pluck them like little burs that prickle the skin before they dig themselves deeper. I embrace you again . . . feel the protection, feel my strength this is yours."*

Tarra: - "I'll remember."

Raphael: - *"Archangel Raphael."*

Tarra: - "Hello."

Raphael: - *"Beloved one how deep is the healing; how deep. How long lasting, how potent is your abilities. Throughout the eons you have and always will use your abilities as a healer. Simply by being in the same room as another you may heal. You look too often to the surface looking for proof of your abilities. The healing goes deeper than this throughout the layers of people's fears and hopes, just like we hold our foreheads against yours, our kisses on your forehead so too does the energy travel from you to others, this kiss of healing, of acceptance, of love . . . just representations of the connection between you and all beings."*

Mother Mary: - "Beloved Tarra, its Mother Mary once more. Feel our love surround you. Feel your ancestors surround you with their support and love also. Your mother is amongst those, she is here with us. She thanks you for your forgiveness."

Tarra: - "You're welcome."

Mother Mary: - "She tells you your new home is not far away. She says it will be bright and sunny to help lift your heart. Saanu will be happy there."

Tarra: - "That's good."

Mother Mary: - "She too kisses your forehead and your cheeks. Tarra we're letting you go now but we are never letting you go and I understand that you understand what we are saying."

Tarra: - "Yes, thank you." (Saanu begins to bark.)

Mother Mary: - "Blessings dear heart . . ."

Tarra: - "Bless you all."

Mother Mary: - "Oh little Saanu is excitable."

Tarra: - "Yes."

Caz and I did two more sessions after my move to Goonellabah Lismore. The first was initiated in answer to a question I had concerning the information I had given Gregory where I felt I may have had my information back to front. The channel was a sort of a welcome to my new home family affair.

4 December, 2006

MERLIN

Tarra: - "Oh! Hello."

Merlin: - "Hello Tarra I see you've finally made your home your own."

Tarra: - "Yes, how are you?"

Merlin: - "Ah busy, busy, all these eons all these dimensions at once sometimes it gets a bit much for one."

Tarra: - Yes, I guess it does when you're totally conscious of what's going on."

Merlin: - "Mmm, sometimes I don't know how conscious I am. . . I feel rather unconscious or . . . dizzy . . . would be the thing. Sometimes I yearn for 3rd dimensional life once again however that was a very long time ago or was it the future."

Tarra: - "Well wherever . . . or whenever."

Merlin: - "I am here in . . . or . . . to answer your call rather about the energy you spoke of earlier."

Tarra: - "Oh, yes."

Merlin: - "What was it again that you wanted?"

Tarra: - "You're speaking about the conversation I had another time with Gregory and I was saying to him that, when we came into physical being we slowed our energy down or slowed our vibration down to become three dimensional. I was wondering if that was reversed or whether that was a different terminology. I'm just . . . I'm a bit confused."

Merlin: - "Yes, yes, yes it's reversed really; it's faster – vibrating very fast. But then again . . . . . (with a sigh). . . . ."

Tarra: - "Yes?" (I should have remembered this.)

Merlin: - "There's soooo many different aspects to this energy thing, it's allllllll in the viewing really. I've got to the point now where I just . . . mmm . . . trust it's as it should be which seems to answer most questions but not many people are happy when that's my answer."

Tarra: - "Well no, but when . . . I think the answer is correct but when you're speaking about faster vibration or slower vibration, if you just be . . ."

Merlin: - "Mmm see, yes."

Tarra: - "Then, you can actually feel the balance."

Merlin: - "That's right. However . . . . . mmm . . ."

Tarra: - ". . . . . it's also like the center of a cyclone or . . . ."

Merlin: - "Ah see, now you're thinking."

Tarra: - "Like a void, it's like suspension."

Merlin: - "I believe there's a saying 'all or nothing'."

Tarra: - "Please explain that . . . (laughing) that's a bit . . ."

Merlin: - "It's always either one or the other. It's all those polar opposites and yet all is the same."

Tarra: - (Magnetics? Is how particles and waves work? Is he talking about particles and waves?) "Yes, there's a light that I want to buy and . . . that is a Buddha light with a black frame and glass outer and that's by . . . what do you call it when you have the opposite ends of the magnets . . . to hold it suspended in mid-air? That's what it feels like . . . well that is what I think it feels like."

Merlin: - *"Yes, yes, positive and negative, nothing exists that doesn't have a positive and negative."*

Tarra: - "True."

Merlin: - *"People tend to forget this. You cannot have a storm without the eye of the storm; cannot have a tree without the roots of the tree; everything has its opposite or hidden part shall we say."*

Tarra: - "And you? What's your opposite?"

Merlin: - *"Mmm, just a moment while I check my drawers . . . I don't think I want to look at my opposite."*

Tarra: - "But you ARE all."

Merlin: - *"Absolutely . . . !"*

Tarra: - "So, if you don't . . . if you stay in balance you don't need to look at the opposite." (Looking at the opposite will manifest that and take us out of balance – many of us are expert at doing this. In other words focusing on what we want to change manifests the very thing we don't want which is why Quan Yin et al were speaking of just being and allowing which keeps us in balance.)

Merlin: - *"Mmm that's correct, it's only when you are more of one than the other that you need to look at the other and be reminded."*

Tarra: - "True."

Tarra: - "So, I recently had an aura photograph taken and I know this is very rudimentary."

Merlin: - *"Oh lovely, very lovely . . ."*

Tarra: - "It's very interesting, it freaked me out actually."

Merlin: - "'freaked me out.' I love this expression."

Tarra: - "Well I was."

Merlin: - "I've been freaked out quite a bit."

Tarra: - "Well it (the photo) was very dark and I sort of thought Oh! . . . Where am I?"

Merlin: - "Mmm, I spent some time as a scientist in the 60's. Don't think I need to say anymore really. Mmm, that freaked me out."

Tarra: - "Oh, if you were a scientist in the 60's did you try all of those drugs?"

Merlin: - "One had to experiment on the mind. That's what it was all about."

Tarra: - "I didn't do this."

Merlin: - "Well, I'm glad that you didn't. It means you are still more in tact than most, more balanced than most."

Tarra: - "But also a little bit more boring than most . . ."

Merlin: - "Ah, this is a delusion, a delusion . . . you're in self-delusion. No, seeing you more balanced than most and that's not boring at all."

Tarra: - "Ok. Now in regards to the aura, can you answer my questions about it? Everything seems in balance in the colours and radiating out . . . it seems to be radiating out not coming in. That's the one thing I see and on the outer edge, the very outer edge, sort of out from my shoulders there's this red on both sides. Now if it's radiating out and that's the passion – red is the passion from what I understand – is that also going to come in."

Merlin: - "What you can't see because the colours are so bright is that the red is there throughout yourself to both sides."

Tarra: - "Ah, ok."

Merlin: - *"This is also a reflection of the pillars of truth."*

Tarra: - "Ok, so Caz was talking about it looking like someone was on either side of me."

Merlin: - *"Yes you could see it as guides and guardians because certainly you have those there. The pillars of truth however represent the polar opposites once again and in that you are perfectly balanced. You have recently done some work that has balanced out many shifts."*

Tarra: - "Yes."

Merlin: - *"Yes and it has come at the time when it is meant to come and it is happening for many here on earth and beyond. Ah . . . huh . . . we could go into the fact that there is no beyond; that there is no earth; soooo much . . . so many different aspects and perspectives."*

Tarra: - "Yes." We stuck to terminology that is familiar to us because there are no words that can adequately describe what 'is'.

Merlin: - *"But you know exactly what I mean and there is no need to go over all that."*

Tarra: - "No."

Merlin: - *"What is important is what you feel in the moment, what we all feel in the moment. Word is powerful, thought is powerful and I know we've been over that before and you understand how important this is to me how powerful the words are that we use. Even for myself at this point where I am where I have a great understanding of transcending all, word . . . well, in the beginning there was the word. I don't think I need to say more."*

Tarra: - "No, possibly not, but now . . . . recently, in a reading that Caz and I were doing - a channel and I can't remember who it was who said "there is no thought", is the word the result of thought or are we sort of speaking from a 3ʳᵈ dimensional perspective when we use word and thought."

Merlin: - "It's a bit like the chicken and the egg, the word is the manifestation of the thought and the thought is the precognition of the word. You cannot have one without the other and yet understanding the form into which we put thought is, what creates . . . what manifests our desires. This is what is most important. Thoughts may not appear to be something that can be controlled but over time this can be done."

Tarra: - "So . . . that is true or pull yourself back from things umm . . . you have to consciously . . . I find at the moment that I still have to consciously do that . . . now I've forgotten what I was going to say."

Merlin: - "May I just say that an example of this thought process, the way some people think would be (X) and others and anybody else that you meet, their thought processes have been ingrained over time through their environment and things they have experienced. They get settled into a way of thought. It's very hard for them to see other people's ways of thought and to understand them or to even want to understand them. There's a certain safety in the pattern of thought that we have."

Tarra: - "Yes, and I understand that."

Merlin: - "It is when they realize that this is happening quicker for most people with the use of various tools that have become more public in recent years. When they realize how powerful the thought and the word is, how their every waking moment is controlled by their own thought and word not anybody else's, that's when their lives can shift. It is those who believe themselves powerless; to be victims; to be pawns who constantly think that they are at the mercy of other people's thoughts, words and intents. When they let go of this process and realize that it is their own thoughts and words that they are at the mercy of the shift can occur and it is instantaneous."

Tarra: - "Mmm . . ."

Merlin: - "One thing will happen and then another will happen and another and yes, they will shift back and forward. It will take a while for some people and others quicker."

Tarra: - "It's taken a while for me."

(There was a segment personal to others of my family omitted here.)

Tarra: - "We had a little bit more to talk about this time."

Merlin: - "Restful . . . farewell Tarra . . ."

Tarra: - "Thank you."

This second channel I felt was basically letting me know that members of the team were adhering to my wishes concerning channeling and would now help me to overcome my blocks but they weren't going to necessarily buy into any thing else. In other words they were going to help me to stay focused on where my attention needed to be if I were to go forward from the point I had already reached. In this channel Quan Yin offers advice about blocks and patterns of behaviour that many of us hold in common and therefore can all benefit from. I squirm as I listen to this but include portions of it anyway.

> **"Argue for your limitations and sure enough, they're yours."**
>
> **Richard Bach**

22 March, 2007

QUAN YIN

Caz: - " . . . . *I can feel a couple sort of there, back on my left side, behind . . . like they're standing there but, I don't know, perhaps you can try asking questions to see if they'll come forward. Try to ask what you really want to know and just see, in this quiet space, what comes up inside you."*

Tarra: - "Well I've asked this question and nothing has come up inside me so . . . in space, the dark between the stars is teeming with life, what are we talking about with life there and is that the dark that when the light touches . . . is the state for creation?"

Caz: - "What are your feelings around that; what's . . . ."

Tarra: - "I'm not getting anything. They (may be) trying to tell me but I'm not getting anything so I'll ask now that they come through and talk to us . . . the appropriate one to answer that question."

Caz: - "I have a feeling that Quan Yin is here but she won't . . . um . . . she won't speak through me if you know what . . . I mean she's saying that um . . . **"She is not here to answer those questions"** *and that she's showing me like a physical block; like in terms of . . . it almost looks like a block with two . . . like a heavy wood and metal block with two nuts on either end that's screwed down tight. And, it's like it's over your chakras . . . its not showing um . . . they mainly seem to be low chakras; its not over your high chakras but over your root and sacral chakra and . . . this is the basis of the block that you have around this area in terms of letting information flow through. It's interesting that it's in the lower ones not in the higher ones."*

Tarra: - "Well not so, most are concerned with survival/fight or flight."

Caz: - "She says **"this is part of the ego seat as well where our ego fights us"** *and that's where . . . yes like we're being tied back . . . feel like we're too heavy to take the information in; like we're too heavy to go up higher . . . your* *not but that's the feeling. And she's saying* **"that's also tied to past lives where you're repeatedly told by priests that such thinking is beyond what's necessary for someone of your station and that this is why it's come up for you as an ego question"**. *You know as it (has) come up in different circumstances for you where you feel like your being put in your place or told you can't do certain things because you know it's not true! You can do anything you want but because of these lives you have an instant reaction when people say these things because you knew it wasn't true back then either but the priests told you where everything revolved around the earth and the earth was flat and all the rest."*

Tarra: - "Yes, however it would appear to be . . . in with ego . . . it would appear to be self-esteem and resentment issues as well in there or is that basically ego."

Caz: - "Basically within . . . ego contains all those things in that, that's how it manifest itself in a physical manner and for you its like a last ditch defense. You know that there are . . . a lot of the beliefs you had in the past are not true anymore and your ego is having trouble struggling to hold onto those beliefs because it's all it has ever known and it wants to stop you from seeking further. So it'll involve itself in this . . . petty little rises . . . the word she keeps giving me is **'rises'**, *like it makes your blood rise. It makes you feel angry and then you hit a wall. It's like you're angry that you've been told you can't because you feel that you can but because you've been told that you can't part of you questions and says what if I can't? Who am I to think? And, this is constantly happening; this constant internal war and dialogue where most of it's subconscious."*

Tarra: - "Yes."

Caz: - "She's showing me . . . using a heavy wrench . . . it's quite a funny picture actually Quan Yin doing this with a heavy wrench, loosening the bolts on this block but she's saying **"they're very rusty (laughing) and that you have to help out with that; that you've got to lubricate those and finally release them yourself."** *So it's a thing for you to visualize and to ask yourself what the rust is from; why is it so stiff; what do you fear that's stopping you from releasing that block? Either . . . that you fear that if you fully recognize* *that we are all one and that you are all one and that you have everything you need that others won't need you or that you won't need others and that you will be alone."*

Tarra: - "But I am alone."

Caz :- "Ah but you're not . . . (laughing freely) . . . she's saying . . . she's laughing at you . . . she's saying that **"she understands why you're saying that because you're also saying that if one person is everything and all things then we're also alone and that you're also physically alone but that you keep creating this perception."**

Tarra: - "What perception?"

Quan Yin: - "That you're fully alone instead of being full and fully one; you're putting the 'al' in there."

Tarra: - "Well . . ."

Caz: - "She said **"this is part of the block that you have . . . that is very rusty . . . this block that you have to be alone; that you rejoice in being aloneness; that you don't want to be alone; all this is all rolled into one and it has been a theme through many lives"** *she's saying and that's why it's hard. This block, it looks like it's something off an ancient ship, almost, you know. It's that old and weathered this wood; it's that hard it's like petrified wood." (For the first fifty years of this life I was rarely alone and often wished for some down time but this is not the type of alone time that Quan Yin is talking about.)*

Tarra: - "Actually in a recent crystal reading petrified wood came up for me."

Caz: - "Yes?"

Tarra: - "Well, I haven't managed to access through the gate into (many of) my past lives and I actually . . . although I'm interested . . . I don't want to get . . . I just want to release things from there without necessarily getting into it because . . . one of the things is . . . you can get waylaid in things that are of no consequence."

Caz: - "Yes, yes bogged down in details."

Tarra: - "Yes in details but by the same token if you don't . . . sometimes you have to know in order to release. I'm not really interested in knowing at the same time . . . I'm interested in having the wisdom and knowledge from my past lives but not necessarily (all). I don't want to reject the lessons either; I want to incorporate it all and that is what I have been trying to do – like the fears and negativities and that sort of thing and embracing what it's taught me."

Caz: - "She's laughing still she says **"this is typical from the star system that you are from. Everything is very logical and that you'd rather seek for higher information than . . . base information."** *She's saying* **"you'd rather avoid the emotional decisions that you've made and learn the whys and wherefores of the Universe but avoid the emotional questions."** *And she's saying* **"you don't have to go back into particular past lives but recognizing the patterns is essential in releasing. It doesn't mean you have to go back and look at all of them but just asking of, "what are my patterns?""** *And the pattern that she is showing is one of aloneness, perceiving your 'self to be alone even when surrounded by people and this is throughout lives. She's showing me this particular one where you're male and there's the priest . . . and it's like you work like . . . an apothecary . . . but you are always seeking for more information but you're shunning the people in your life who want to be with you physically both in a sexual relationship and in family relationships. You're always seeking for higher information and this priest is saying no that's not for you, you're to work day to day and do God's work day to day. You don't need these higher answers which you know is not right and you want them. There's a reason why you want them. You want the answers but because you keep seeking outside for the answers you're not allowing the intimate relationships to really take hold. That's that particular life and they're showing me other ones where . . . one of you as a young girl . . . seems to be in the 1800's or something . . . like as if you're going to church . . . pretty little clothes and dresses. But, you're only about four and you're chucking a* *tantrum, stamping your foot and saying nobody loves me, no-one pays attention to anything that I want. Your mothers got this shocked look on her face . . . she's quite elegant . . . but what flashes through her head is you cuddled up on her lap and her reading to you and your father teaching you how to write with a feathered quill and a fountain pen and different things. And . . . your sister teaching you to skip and everyone working with you but you in this petulant moment of being four you are convinced that you're alone. She's showing me that it's not just you that has this theme but so often many of us do and it comes from the feeling of disconnection which is why we're always seeking to go back and why we're always seeking to go higher and to reconnect with all that is. But . . . we still want to be put up higher and . . . not necessarily on a pedestal but someone to recognize us for who we are and to say yes you are special; you have these wonderful talents; you are such a great help; you are unique. All those things are true they are a part of the search and it is understandable to have those thoughts and to also deny them and to feel angry when those thoughts arise – angry at oneself and angry at others who make them rise. She keeps on saying this 'rise'; it's very important, it's like a kundalini, almost."*

Tarra: - Well it's important for these things to rise for us to work on. That's what this ascension is about."

Caz: - "Yes."

Tarra: - "But the interesting thing is I think and tell people how marvelous they are because I think they are but I don't seem to get that back . . ."

Caz: - "Yes."

Tarra: - ". . . and after fifty-six years it's a bit tiring. There are times when I get that back and I don't mean that I give out and expect back or anything like that but sometimes you need . . . you need to understand that."

Caz: - "Yes."

Tarra: - "But also I understand, having been a manager of people that you can tell them everything they're doing right and there's one thing that needs some work and that's the one thing they'll resent and hate you for . . . so I understand the psychology of that too. And, I thought I was sort of . . . releasing a lot of that and a lot more self-love and all that sort of thing . . . I thought I was dealing with that."

Caz: - "Yes, you have to um . . . Quan Yin's showing me the picture of the Taro card. I think it's the nine of staves, with a person with . . . it feels like almost a fort up around them (that) they've built, expecting to have to defend oneself."

Tarra: - "Oh well, that's often been (the case)."

Caz: - *"Yes, and that's put up and then again she's showing me the wood of that and the wood of the block, she says* **"there's no blame, that's just the way things are; everybody has their pattern and more than you know have the same pattern. It's all part of moving back into oneness and the ego holding on to that last thing of wanting to be separate; that even while we are one we're still unique."** *I can't fully understand that but this is what she's saying that even though we're all one we're still unique."*

Tarra: - "Well, that's because the energy is ah . . . is that sort of to do with particles and waves type energies, the illusiveness of the energies that must flow through everything? Does that make sense?"

Caz: - *"Yes, she's agreeing and she's showing it. She saying* **"it's like all the little molecules and the space that is perceived to be between the molecules is God and that we see ourselves as flowing separately surrounded by God but not within. Not truly within God and not breaking ourselves down to the small and realizing that there is no difference and we are more aware of it."** *But, she's saying that* **"it's been so long, so many patterns and lives on earth where we haven't been taught that, that it's very difficult to assimilate it fully.""**

Tarra: - "It's um . . . the most comfortable place I find myself . . . and I can feel myself shake off the restrictions of the smallness of my being as opposed to the greatness of my divine being and by that I mean . . . in the perceived feeling of release and size. I often can't . . . I feel like I'm being weighed down on the shoulders and I can't stay within my body like that quite often and I stretch out and almost shake . . . and go right out so that I become the Universe, in body form as well but, in energy form. I don't know if I'm making sense there?"

Caz: - "Absolutely, she's saying that **"you've been doing that more and more and that's wonderful. To keep going with that because that's what's helping to loosen the nuts on your block . . . just allowing yourself to let things flow and to flow into your mind what you feel you want to do. Not to worry about what should I do; how should I do it; why certain things are happening – just flow."**

Tarra: - "Mmm"

Caz: - "Now she's showing me the Ganges and she's saying or showing rather, it flowing through the mountains all crystal clear and beautiful, and then . . . that it's still being a holy (river), so holy no matter what's in it."

Tarra: - "I actually, it's interesting, I smelt the Ganges the other day and it came up in a thought of mine. It has a particular smell on the plains and on the Terai and it must have been something coming through that someone was trying to tell me about. Anyway, it's interesting that you bring it up now."

Quan Yin: - "The Ganges represents the river of life to the Hindu people and it is very important that you focus on the river of life, the flow. That is how all energy works; all energy is flowing it is never stagnant – it is never, ever stagnant. It may appear to be stagnant but it is never . . . there is always change occurring."

Tarra: - "I often um . . . I don't know whether I visualize or I actually go out but I'll use the word visualize . . . storms and lightning and the wind and the rain going through me and it's a really lovely feeling. And I . . . huh . . . this is a contradiction in terms but . . . trying to step aside from this and allowing the flow and I never seem to come up against a wall where . . . when it's in the elements . . . where I love the water and all that and the rain and the energy of the storms and the thunder and all of that and I never get afraid when I'm doing that. I never think oh, you can't do that and stop it or get hit by lightning or run into a tree or anything like that."

Caz: - "I can't feel her. It's like she's just gone and I don't know what you last said I heard the 'running into a tree' and something I think about 'lightning' and I just went. I don't know where I went."

Tarra: - "That's Ok."

Caz: - "No, it feels weird so I'd like to hear what you were just saying?"

Tarra: - "I was talking about when she was talking about the river of life. When they do that, I never know when they go like that, I never know if I've done something wrong; if I've lost them through something (said). Anyway, I was talking about . . . after she said the Ganges is the river of life and to allow the energies to flow through . . . that's probably why she has gone to allow the energies to flow through. I often see, not so much visualize as actually be there . . . but as I said to her I'll call it visualizing being out totally with the storm and the lightning and the rain and things just flowing through me and when I do that I never come up against fear where I get hit by lightning or run into a tree or anything like that. I just float . . . a bit like . . . you remember the channel with Gregory where he was talking about having traveled with Matthew Flinders energetically?"

Caz: - "Ah, I'd forgotten about that."

Tarra: - "Yes and I do that all the time and I don't know whether I travel with anyone but I love the elements and that's what I was saying when we lost her."

*Caz: - "You know I think that's why . . . . huh . . . it's almost like she's gone over the mountain and she's calling back **"yes that's it!"** that's why she went because that's exactly it, what you were talking about . . . that's the information. That's the best way for the information to come through for you. The visualizing yourself out there and letting it flow. Where you go next is your answers."*

Tarra: - "Ok."

Caz: - *"And then you sit and do your 'blog' on the computer or write it out or whatever."*

Tarra: - "Mmm and as you say, don't ask questions. (I'll never learn! I pose another question.) There is one thing I need to ask about the old energy/ new energy thing and that is: You see a numbers come up . . . . like I often see 244, 255, 233, 333, 444, all those things and I often wonder if the messages we receive that were written last century . . . whether they're still appropriate as messages from spirit or are they messages from the 'self'? Have they always been messages from 'self' or does spirit . . . and when I say spirit like Quan Yin, Archangel Michael, and all of those . . . get involved in those messages for support?"

Caz: - *"(Laughing) I'm getting . . . huh . . . they're saying **"mixed-messages is the best way to describe it . . . some messages are from the self and some messages are from spirit and that often ego interferes with the self with it. And, that's all throughout the bible and old channelings as well, that there's a mix. They are just slipping in and out all the time.""***

"Tarra: - "Yes, so it's difficult when you're still dealing with . . . Archangel Michael (it was Jesus who asked me that not Michael) asked me ages ago why I was concerned with ego but it seems to me that I need to be concerned – not concerned but dealing with it."

Caz: - *"I think it's being aware . . . I think that we have to be aware that ego is a part of ourselves; ego is like the barrier that we built up to protect ourselves when we came into this dimension and this earth."*

Tarra: - "Mmm, but there's a negative and a positive side to ego though"

Caz: - *"Yes, absolutely that's what I mean; the negative and positive thing to defense; the barrier that we built up around ourselves to protect us and to help us with the completely different energies that we have to deal with here."*

Tarra: - "Yes."

Caz: - "It's not self-aware it just is; it's like a fungus that decides to grow and fungi can be good and it can be bad. It's just there to protect us and make us think about things and whether or not we need to . . . can we push past that or are we happy to stay in that."

Tarra: - "Well if it's balanced ego. Spirit has ego (or at least the Ascended Masters do); they seem to have the same things that we have; they just have it in balance from what I perceive."

Caz: - "Yes, I just think it became more . . . . dense here, you know."

Tarra: - "Yes."

Quan Yin had gone and Caz and I were speculating as we always do when we are together so I'll finish this session at this point.

PART THREE

CHAPTER 11

INDIVIDUALITY

I first wrote the following article for publication in response to an invitation from the founder of a self growth website. It reflects the beliefs I hold for myself. Reading it over, before posting it on the website, I decided to include it here instead. I do not think it appropriate to change its tone and prefer to present it here as it was originally intended.

'INDIVIDUALITY'

"Reading after a certain age diverts the mind too much from its creative pursuits. Any man who reads too much and uses his own brain too little falls into lazy habits of thinking"

Albert Einstein

It would be nice to believe we are a product of our environment and to a large degree this would seem to be the case. However, we actually make choices and have reactions to what we see, hear, read and feel around us – the things that make up our environment. Therefore it seems to me that we are a product of our own choices. We adopt those beliefs, moral codes and practices which resonate with our own thoughts and feelings and discard those that don't. Our subconscious mind does this at lightening speed without end. Have you ever paused in your life to wonder how you came to believe some of the things you do and why you accepted them without question? Our beliefs are constantly updated as we learn and experience through living our lives. The more we experience the greater our compassion becomes for others as they go through the traumas and joys of their lives. The more we experience the less we judge because we understand the strength and trust in ourselves that is required to make choices. Ultimately the more we experience the more we honour our own and other people's choices.

It is not only those of us who put our thoughts to paper, lecture, paint, dance, compose music, produce movies and documentaries, etc who have ground breaking thoughts, ideas, and ways of relating to the world we see around us. The composite 'I' that is the individual needs no validation from any outside source. As each of us experiences; observes and creates; we evolve into more complex beings always understanding that there is more to learn until we reach the point where it becomes apparent that it is not necessarily about learning but about knowing. This is the intuitive side of our nature which resonates with or rejects ideas and beliefs and with expanded awareness is strengthened to the point where it becomes very difficult to hide our heads in the sand and say when things go wrong "I had no idea that this or that would happen as a result of my action or inaction."

Have you ever had someone ask you a question and, until you answered, were not aware that you actually had an opinion on the subject let alone a response? Did you find yourself wondering afterwards where you could possibly have gained that insight? We need to nurture this side of our nature and as we do this our trust in ourselves will grow. This innate ability is our barometer setting the stage for personal empowerment. Isolated individuals and groups have always known this and acted on the knowledge but humanity as a whole has not done so before. More and more individuals are doing so now and as a result critical mass has been reached pulling us up into a heightened world consciousness.

Many of those interested in the subject of 'self growth' say there is a revolution going on and I agree. There is a quiet revolution occurring on our planet. More and more individuals are making up their own mind about what is going on around them and not relying on an outside source to interpret it for them. This is occurring in every walk of life from the scientific to the religious; from government to community; from the professional to the lay person. The 'new agers' is already an obsolete term. Have you ever noticed that strange feeling you get in the pit of your stomach, that jolt, when something you hear is inaccurate or incomplete? We should heed those times of knowing and learn to trust ourselves. We have this innate ability to recognize the truth of a situation so we need to be the skeptical observer. The truth will surface much faster than it has done in the past and it will become obvious to the awakened observer that the jolt they felt came from their inner knowing. We are all connected.

Humanity has reached this point and accepts that growth and evolution is ever expanding. There is no end to it not even when we graduate to the next level, to heaven, or whatever our personal beliefs are. The latest scientific discovery is only the forerunner to what is yet to be discovered. The latest insight into the ascension process is only the forerunner to where we have yet to explore. Consciousness is ever expanding and even the Ascended Masters have their growth on their own ascension paths. This knowledge is staring us in the face now and has a greater impact on our understanding than ever before. Many of us are paralyzed by it believing we are unable to respond as we should; believing that we don't know what to do; believing we will not be heard; believing we are too insignificant to count. This is not the case. It does not matter if others hear us or not, it only matters that we hear and trust ourselves when we express a personal truth.

We as individuals and as a world society have the ability to respond to affect change not only in our personal lives and community but on the world stage. All that is needed is to expend our energy on the things that matter to us. This focus automatically withdraws our support from the things that don't. Each individual has the ability to do this and the freedom to choose how they will use their energy. Here is a simple example of how this can be done. *"If I do not believe in resolving issues by going to war it is much more effective to advocate peace than it is to demonstrate against war. In doing this I would be using the positive side of my energy to reinforce peace and be placing it squarely on my desired outcome."*

As we stretch our senses to reach new and greater understanding we encounter more refined energies and meet new ways to interact with the environment of our world. We also understand that what we do here has a ripple effect on our Universe and beyond. Energy is constantly on the move flowing through everything and everyone. We go from centuries of making things happen by manipulation, to allowing things to happen through intent. This is quite a shift for the individual let alone humanity. Integrity and positive thinking are the tools needed to live life in these expanded energies. My excitement comes from wondering as I expand my consciousness and reach out or into my senses "what wonders will I encounter next?"

We find ourselves in a new world where our expanded awareness necessitates that now, more than ever, we take responsibility for our actions in the wider community of which we are a part. Our thoughts and actions have far reaching effects as our power to create is strengthened by this expanded awareness. Our increased power carries with it the need to be very clear about what we want to bring into being. We cannot afford to be careless with our thoughts and actions because greater power creates swiftly and with greater precision leaving less and less room for error.

On a personal level we as individuals can also use this expanded awareness of our own abilities to apply our thoughts to healing our own bodies and lives. Changing the way we think can turn our lives around creating abundance in all we touch be it spiritual growth, health, friendships, love, experiences, abilities – abundance in all things. We all have unique abilities which we need to explore if, as individuals, we are so inclined. Our world will become greater when we accept and become all that we can be.

I see two main fears that are stopping most of us (you may see more). The first is that we are afraid to be all that we can be. The second is that we are afraid of what others will say and think. It is much more important and empowering to accept ourselves as we are and trust that we are enough as who we are. The individual does not need the approval of others to validate their authenticity. Everyone counts. It is enough that we are here.

The greatest block to self-empowerment is the one we create in our own minds. That is our own inclination to compare ourselves to others and to see ourselves falling short of who we think we should be. Instead look at the great being that you are and know that you are enough and capable of growing in the character that is you. If we expect everyone to agree with us then we are definitely going to be disappointed. Even our closest friends and family do not necessarily celebrate our expanded growth as we do. For whatever reasons, they may believe they know better and they do for them but they do not for you. Only you know what is right for you.

Our differences are what make our world exciting. We are individual parts of humanity and like the cells of a body we are all necessary. As we believe, think, and do so we create. This has always been the case and if we believe we live in a bad world then, for us as individuals, the world will be a bad one. Energy carries no judgment. Have you ever wondered why some people are so content with their life? It is because that is the life they have created for themselves because that is how they choose to be in their world. Why not try it? How do you want to be in your world?

Blessings

Tarra Logan

CHAPTER 12

FOREVER EVOLVING

Love Conquers All

"Cultivating a close, warm-hearted feeling for others automatically puts the mind at ease and opens our inner door. It helps remove whatever fears or insecurities we may have and gives us the strength to cope with any obstacles we encounter. It is the principle source of success in life."

Dalai Lama

Communications come in many forms. The following is a perfect example of this. I had just finished reading the book 'Care of the Soul' by Thomas Moore. He suggests acknowledging all feelings including the negative ones. He also writes about 'Ancient Mythology' and 'Gods and Goddesses' for each emotion and how all of these impact on our lives. His way of presenting his ideas helped me to understand more fully the advice I received from spirit – "don't deny your humanness".

After reading the book I wrote: - The 'Soul' craves for all of its 'self' to be acknowledged. What does this concept really mean to me? It means – be honest and accepting of my true nature and understand that maintaining balance within my 'Soul' is necessary for my spiritual and physical wellbeing."

I wandered away from my computed and picked up my copy of 'A Guide for the Advanced Soul' by Susan Hayward. The facing pages I opened the book at revealed the following two quotes.

> *"By going along with feelings, you unify your emotional, mental, and bodily states. When you try to fight or deny them, you divorce yourself from the reality of your being."*

> **Jane Roberts**

> *"That which oppresses me is it my soul trying to come out in the open, or the soul of the world knocking at my heart for its entrance?"*

> **Rabindranatii Tagore**

Synchronicity! I love it!

Having special friends who, I know, will not be put off by my thoughts or any subject I wish to broach is so liberating. The following e-mail is an example of one of the ways in which sharing my thoughts and heart supports and helps me remain focused even during the saddest and most challenging of times.

22 September, 2007

Hi

My friend's funeral is on Tuesday afternoon. I am leaving today and will arrive back on Friday afternoon.

I forgot to tell you about two experiences I had.

The first was while I was listening to a communication I was receiving. I thought the entity could be Jesus or Sananda and the reply I heard was **"You ain't nothin' but a hound dog . ."** *and then I knew it was Sananda.*

The second was when I was doing Kuthumis heart chakra activation meditation. I was clearing and I said to myself "I wonder if I cleared it completely" and I heard **"Look at me I'm Sandra Dee"** *and I started laughing as I finished it with them* **"lousy with virginity!"**

That should have given you a good laugh!

A channel by Kuthumi & Pallas Athena may interest you. www.awakening-healing.com *Go to prophesy 2007 and the article is the one in September on '999 ascension this lifetime'.*

Lol

I had been communicating by email with another of my friends about a life change she was contemplating and she ended by saying that perhaps all she needed to do was take a leap of faith. I include part of my response to that here.

"Very well put. Leap of Faith is exactly it. Knowing it and acting on it is often another matter. It brings up the question "In whom do we trust?" and generally we think it is in God, the Universe, someone or something outside ourselves. Actually it is our 'self' who we have to trust and have faith in. Without a doubt we are solely responsible for our choices and that is the truth that many of us won't accept."

One day while sitting at my computer typing my left knee suddenly began to jump and within a couple of seconds shook so violently that I couldn't type, this lasted about a minute and then as suddenly stopped. I'm sure everyone has experienced this however, the reason I mention it is because it reminded me of a couple of things that happen to me so often that they seem normal to me now.

When I am deep in meditation or taking part in the activations particularly those Kuthumi channels through Michelle Eloff on the www. thelightweaver.org web site, while deep in the meditation, I have become conscious of my upper body rocking smoothly and slowly in a small, back and forward motion. Movement helps us to take on higher vibrations.

At other times when I'm laying on my bed the energy of my body will begin a seesaw motion from head to toe. It feels like the bed I'm lying on is a seesaw or like I'm lying in a tub of water and someone has gently bumped the foot of the tub causing the water to ebb and flow head to toe, slowly and smoothly. This one is energetic lasting for up to 5 minutes and my physical body doesn't move at all. I feel like I'm almost floating and my bed feels as soft as I imagine lying on a cloud would be. I like this one the best because it is definite and steady in its motion but very comforting and soothing and I want it to go on forever. This last one occurred several times particularly during the months following my mother's and my brother-in-law's deaths. Was it my own energy attempting to comfort me? I have no idea.

RANDOM THOUGHTS AND ITEMS
OF INTEREST TO PONDER

"We can easily forgive a child who is afraid of the dark; the real tragedy is when men are afraid of the light."

Plato

1. I always remind myself that there is no-one who judges us as harshly as we do ourselves however, others can reinforce our bad opinion of ourselves. All they are doing is holding up a mirror for us to see how we see ourselves. Accept that we are perfect pieces of creation just like a storm is perfect, as is a cloudy sky, or a sunset. Each has its own perfect characteristics as do we.

2. We do not need to change others or have others agree with us. There are as many pathways to ascension as there are entities in the Universe; authentic and uniquely individual. Many are well

along on their path without being aware of their spiritual growth at all. They are instinctively following a process that is unique to them. It is within all of us to do this.

3. There is a perception among some that when we pass over we become spiritual automatically dropping the persona of the life we just left on earth. It is my understanding that we actually retain much of this life's character traits because that aspect of the soul still exists. When we speak to Grandma for example we are speaking to the aspect of her soul that is our Grandma. The soul itself is much bigger than that and is not restricted to just one tiny aspect of itself.

4. We have many barriers that belong to a bygone age. Other people's negative opinions of us that we have taken on board which have accumulated over many life times; vows we have made; memories of traumas endured; beliefs that we have adopted based on faulty information. It is now possible for us to let go of all of these issues and clear Karma simply by making a choice to do so.

5. Agonizing over the question 'what is my purpose?' The answer is not essential however we always want to know. If you are searching, and until you find the answer, take comfort in the fact that each one of us has a purpose at this time. We wouldn't be here if we didn't and we all anchor light on the planet in any case.

6. We often bump up against people who don't believe in our unique authentic process – our perceptions; how we remember and interpret events in our individual life. Others have their own unique life to live. We each have enough of a challenge with our own life without trying to live another's for them believing we are capable of knowing more about their memories and thought processes than they do. That just isn't possible and we can't know about theirs with certainty either.

7. When you meet someone who thinks they are Gods gift to the world and treats you in a condescending manner don't be diverted from your path. That person is Gods gift to the world. It is sad that they have forgotten that you are Gods gift to the world too.

8. In her book **'Conscious Ageing'** *Margo Knox* writes: -

'We can choose to be true to ourselves,
True to our heart,
True to our inner guidance,
True to our source . . . .
or continue to suffer through life experiences.

9. **TWO GIFTS TO SHARE** the first is a wonderful, one minute clip filmed in Glasgow http://www.youtube.com/ watch_popup?v=Hzgzim5m7oU&vq=medium and the second is a philosophers quote/poem: -

'Watch your thoughts; they become words
Watch your words; they become actions;
Watch your actions they become; habits;
Watch your habits; they become character;
Watch your character; it becomes your destiny.'

Lao Tzu

CONCLUSION

"Live in the moment, look within and there you will find all things."

Anon

When I first made contact with Spirit I had filled my body with golden light and sent it down into the center of the earth. Then from its core let it release bursting it out into the Universe in celebration. It was an instinctive action like others I responded to in the past. At the time I had no idea why I did it or even that it could be done. The golden light I had chosen was recognized throughout time as my shingle and the Ascended Masters responded to my light communication.

11 January 2010 How can I convey to you in words where my journey has taken me over the last eight years. I have been dimension hopping to such a degree that focusing on what is now past was impossible for me. Then I went through a long period where the past and what it offered me in experience seemed to matter little. The memories seemed irrelevant and my book stalled at the stage of editing. It took me a while to remember how isolating the ascension journey can be and why I decided to write of my experience in the first place.

2013 I had been doing some development exercises and one of the things I had to do was write about what gives me joy and, as it transpires, that which gives me joy is also what I am grateful for. I did not think or try to form logical sentences; I just let the words flow.

JOY

"The joy I have felt is in having all that I have seen in my travels and all that I have experienced stay with me always. Beautiful sunsets, wonderful people, and fresh cool air like the air I am breathing right now. A warm fire, wonderful sex, a passionate kiss, hitting the right note when I am singing, expressing myself truthfully, laughing with spirit, teasing and being teased, high jumping, dining with friends with laughter, celebration and warmth. Enjoying like interests, enjoying the beauty of my youth, the birds songs. Enjoying watching my dogs - Saanu running and jumping across a puddle; Tinker swimming in the creek and not wanting to get out of the water. Keith whistling to music he loves, Ruth enjoying her garden and roses, John enjoying his rum and coke. My nieces laughing and cuddling, my brothers' smiles, my sister's heart, my Mothers and my Fathers love. Tinker jumping into our arms and playing with his ball, Saanu's love as she was telling me it was time for her to go. My beautiful blue budgerigar as he tried to help me tend to his sick mate by pushing her along the perch toward the medicine I was trying to give her. I marvel at thunder storms, waterfalls, the beauty of the animals and the birds, the rocks and the mountains, the babbling brooks, the snow, an avalanche, and a baby's gurgling laugh; the gentleness of the large carpet snake as I lifted him off the budgie's cage with a broom; a comfortable sunny day, a good movie, a healing cry, a clear glass of water, good cooking, crisp fruit, my heart, my mind, the child who is me, my ego, and my friends. I realize why I am in love with the illusion of our physical life here on Gaia."

The final part of the exercise was to write a letter to myself about what I felt spirit wanted to say to me. I had no hesitation or difficulty with this as it flowed easily onto the page. Did I have help with it? Yes, I believe I did.

"Dear Heart why do you feel alone when we are right here always with you? We saw you today as you enjoyed Julie's meditation; we are here with you now, we are you. The things you admire in us are in you also. The great ease with which you know we can manifest is yours also for you cannot recognize those unless you know they are within you also. We are one and of God – there is no separation. God is all things; within all things he/she has never left you and loves you unconditionally.

You have been wondering what we think of your book whilst at the same time knowing that what we think is irrelevant. Your book is about your experience with the ascension process and therefore can only be written and expressed in one way and that is your way. Ask yourself "what feels right?" and follow your heart. Have no expectations and know that there are no wrong choices. We love you dearly and we honour the path you have chosen; our unconditional love to you Tarra."

Many speak of the following and I have read of it many times and have even said to myself that it is so. Bashar explained it clearly in an audio channel through Darryl Anka on the 8th November 2007 on www.newsforthesoul.com. Daryl was being interviewed by Nicole Whitney founder of that site. The channel can be found along with others of his in the web site Archives. He was speaking of the 'I AM'. I believed it to be true but I didn't know it to be true. I didn't know it to be true until I sat and wrote the following: -

"How did I not see it? I became lost in the process of my journey back to who I am. My heart, emotions, and mind were contorted like a pretzel the majority of the time. As I delved deeper and deeper another aspect of my personality would reveal itself – or so I thought.

What I finally realized is that I was searching in the lessons my soul wished to experience and that they were not me at all. I didn't need to search through the lives that I've lived to find myself. Yet, the paradox is that until I delved into some events of my past I wasn't aware that this indeed was the case. Those lives were just various characters for which my soul fragmented to act its parts. I got so involved in those parts that I thought they were me. They are not me; they are a part of the whole of me – of my soul. Now, as a result of this realization, I have let go of the residue of emotions and hurts resulting from those roles."

The sum total of my experiences enhances my soul. That wisdom when accessed and applied with unconditional love is very powerful indeed.

An absolute abundance of blessings to you all!

Tarra

Printed in the United States
By Bookmasters